Leadership Education:
Developing Skills for Youth

by

William B. Richardson
Louisiana State University

John B. Feldhusen
Purdue University

Trillium Press
Monroe, New York

Trillium Press, Inc.
PO Box 209
Monroe, N.Y. 10950
(914) 783-2999

ISBN: 0-89824-166-9
Printed in the United States of America

Table of Contents

PREFACE

The development of leaders is an important national issue. News reports and national journalists stress the problems associated with the lack of effective leaders in all phases of American life. Educational, religious, political, industrial and community institutions in our society are but a few instances where the lack of effective leaders is noted.

The development of leaders as a national priority requires that the concept of leadership be stressed at an early stage in the education of youth. Leadership education as a curriculum thrust in schools has promise as a field of study much the same as the arts and sciences. Youth who will someday begin to fill the various leadership roles in our society can develop their skills in a non-threatening learning environment.

This book is designed to provide the basic leadership skills needed by youth in leadership education programs. Three important aspects of leadership education are stressed. First, information pertaining to the nature and outcomes of leadership education is presented. Second, leadership from the leader and member perspective is discussed. Third, leadership education from an organization perspective is provided.

This book is based on extensive development and testing by the authors. A project funded in 1975 by the Indiana State Board for Vocational and Technical Education initiated the authors' research in leadership education. The funded project resulted in the development of thirteen leadership education units of instruction. Each unit was extensively tested in Indiana public schools. A doctoral dissertation by Dr. Kevin Hynes further tested and documented the effectiveness of the units. The authors of this book have used these thirteen units in numerous seminars, workshops, and formal classes. The many refinements made in the original units appear in the contents of this book.

Each chapter provides basic information necessary to master the chapter objectives. In order that students gain practical experience in applying the leadership skills, each chapter contains leadership development activities. Also, an additional activities section is included in each chapter to allow students and teachers to gain additional leadership education experiences.

Chapter I

AN INTRODUCTION TO LEADERSHIP EDUCATION

OBJECTIVES

After finishing this chapter, you should be able to:

1. Write a personal definition of leadership.
2. Recognize the qualities of a leader in yourself and in leaders of our country.
3. Compare the three ways that leadership can develop.
4. Recognize the four definitions of leadership demonstrated in speeches given by your classmates.
5. Choose the method of leadership which you feel would work best for you in different situations.
6. Identify an area in your life that has potential for improving your leadership ability.

In the early years of our country, we were fortunate to have many good leaders. Those were difficult years, filled with new challenges and questions around each corner. Many decisions were required concerning the future of the United States. Strong leadership helped make the U.S. a respected and powerful country. Yet, the challenges did not end in 1800, nor in 1900, or 1980. They are still present today. Our country needs strong leaders to make difficult decisions and to answer difficult questions. The issues become a bit more complex each year. Many times, we, as American citizens, feel that our leaders fail to resolve major problems. When this happens, we question their ability to lead our country.

Our nation's leadership is not limited to our political offices such as the President, the Congress, governors or representatives. Businessmen are leaders in the area of commerce. Teachers are leaders in the field of education. Ministers are leaders in the realm of religion. Any field of human endeavor is represented by its leaders, including the creative areas of art, music and literature. Even research, exploration, and technology require creative leadership. Each person is faced with leadership whether it be in church, schools, business, or in the home.

LEADERSHIP

Leadership may be formal, as in an elected or appointed leader of an organization. Leadership may also be informal, as in the case of the person who has influence in a group as a specialist or advisor, though he/she does not hold an elected position.

As you read this chapter, keep in mind: 1) If civilization is to progress, we must have leaders. 2) Leaders do not just happen. In order to become a leader, the person must inherit the position, win it in some manner, or be appointed to it. Usually some training is required. 3) The stability of a group or organization depends on its leadership. Leadership is a concern for all. The future of our country depends on our elected officials and on the decisions which they make. Your future may depend on your ability to lead.

WHAT IS IT?

Leadership is an ability which may lead to a better job, to more security and self-confidence, and to greater service to society as a whole. A leader is someone who stands out in a group because he/she possesses, to an unusual degree, some outstanding qualities. These qualities may be valued, respected, or feared by those people who follow the leader. The first of those qualities might be *superior skill* as demonstrated by the quarterback of a football team. Because he has the skill to lead the team and set up scoring plays, his leadership and skill is respected. Closely related to superior skill is the *quality of knowledge*. People will usually follow someone who is knowledgeable in an area. This may easily be seen by observing the professionals in a field whose job is to offer expert advice to the general population. Examples of this type of leadership might be doctors, lawyers, ministers, and teachers. Another quality which might be possessed by a leader is *personal position*. The office of president or governor or the position of king or queen commands a certain amount of respect. The degree of respect will depend on how much leadership ability the person possesses. One other characteristic which may produce a leader is financial wealth. A wealthy person may use his/her finances to help others and thus he/she becomes a benevolent leader. In some cases, money can be used to buy power.

Leadership is a composite of these four qualities. Individual leaders will possess varying degrees of each quality.

FOUR DEFINITIONS OF LEADERSHIP

Leadership may be defined as *personality*. The person who possesses the greatest number of traits, behaviors, or characteristics that a group considers desirable will usually be the leader of that group. Because the group is impressed by the personality of their leader, he/she is able to influence the group to the greatest degree. For example, if a group elects a leader who is confident, humorous, popular, etc., then that group probably defines leadership as personality. This leader

4

may or may not have the ability to be a good leader, even though he or she possesses some of the personality characteristics of a leader.

Have you noticed persons in your school who have very pleasing and assertive personalities? Most all schools have these individuals. Such persons can make good use of their personalities to become leaders within the school. Pause now and think of some students in your school whose personalities have helped them become good leaders.

Leadership may also be defined as a form of *persuasion*. Persuasive leaders have great ability to convince or inspire others to follow their directions, orders, or commands. The persuasive leader relies on verbal ability and rhetorical skills rather than personality traits. This is not to say that this type of leader may not have a pleasing personality, but the talent lies chiefly in the ability to "inspire people to action."

The third definition of leadership is referred to as the *power relation*. In this definition, the person with the highest rank and the greatest amount of power will be the leader of the group. An historical example of leadership as a power relation is the Roman concept of the pater familias. The pater familias (or father of the family) was the leader of the clan and had the power of life or death over the family members. Leadership as a power relation is present today in the form of representative democracy in which we elect officials to represent us. In this process, we grant these officials the power to make major decisions which will affect our lives.

The fourth definition of leadership involves *initiating action and maintaining structure*. In this type of leadership, the person who initiates the action and seeks to maintain the structure of the group toward an established goal will be the leader of the group. A private citizen organizes a group to fight for better schools. He or she initiates the action, develops a following, and then maintains the structure of the group as it pursues its goals of school improvement.

These definitions of leadership can be very similar to one another and tend to overlap. The leadership qualities exhibited by a particular leader will often include a combination of all four.

Most of you will not be faced with leadership situations like the president or prime minister or even congresssman. But it will be helpful to you, whatever the level of leadership you achieve, to know well the nature and characteristics of the good leader.

THREE WAYS LEADERSHIP DEVELOPS

We have discussed some definitions of leadership and some qualities of a leader so far. Although we know that the major factor of leadership is the ability to influence people, we do not necessarily know exactly how leadership develops. One way leadership develops is called the great person explanation. The great person theory of leadership goes back to the days when kings and queens were considered to be superior to the rest of society. In American society, we also tend to see the President as a great and possibly superior person. Of course, if the President fails as a leader, we are also quite willing to change our view. In fact, if his behavior warrants it, a president can even be removed from office. Looking back at a few famous leaders such as Alexander the Great, Julius Caesar, Oliver Cromwell, Abraham Lincoln, Franklin Delano Roosevelt, and Winston Churchill, we see that they all demonstrated high levels of greatness that made them effective leaders.

The second way leadership can develop is based on environmental or situational conditions. The social conditions of a group, for example, may determine who the leader of the group will be. Because there is a great deal of stress, conflict, or unrest in a certain population, the person who offers the greatest hope or the best solution to a problem will become the leader of the group. This person may not be able to solve the problems at all, but he/she will still be offered the position of leader. This concept might be more easily understood by looking at the men who emerged as leaders following the Great Depression of 1929. While Roosevelt, Churchill, and Hitler showed themselves to be powerful leaders, Benito Mussolini became little more than a second rate leader. Mussolini did not demonstrate the qualities that make a "great leader." Rather, we see him as someone who took advantage of an already bad situation. Leaders of this type represent environmental or situational explanations of leadership.

The final way leadership develops is not singular in nature, but rather attempts to unite the first two explanations. The personal situation explanation of leadership says that strong leaders develop when their ability can be used to remedy a specific situation. Usually, great leaders develop during times of stress, conflict or unrest. The interaction of the personality of the leader and the demands of the situation determine the type of leadership that results.

Mary is an illustration of a personal situational leader. Mary is a member of the Honor Club in East High School. She arrived at the car wash that the Honor Club was sponsoring to raise money for their trip to Washington, D.C. The president of the club, Bob Smith, was upset. Nothing was going as planned. Cars were arriving from three directions. Jack forgot the hoses, and there weren't enough towels to go around. Mary quickly suggested that Jack should go to her house, which was only five blocks away, to pick up her father's hose. She next suggested that they park cars in two of the driveways to stop cars from pulling in from different directions. She finally suggested that the club sponsor check with school officials to see if towels from the athletic department could be used if members of the honor club assumed responsibility for their return. The car wash ran smoothly the remainder of the day. Mary kept calm and was able to think quickly in order to salvage a bad situation. She provided the proper leadership.

Mary's leadership did not come about because she was a great person. She sized up the situation, assertively suggested appropriate action, and assisted in implementing a revised plan based on the conditions at hand.

In the above illustration, what method of leadership did Mary exhibit? Did she act as a boss or have a "don't care" attitude? No, she demonstrated a very effective leadership method. But, what are the methods of leadership?

THREE METHODS OF LEADERSHIP

There are three methods of leadership with which you are probably familiar, even though you do not know terms for them. They are autocratic, laissez faire, and democratic.

An *autocratic* or authoritarian leader is characterized as determining all policies, dictating and directing how to do things, and deciding the activities for the members of the group. Perhaps the best example of an autocratic leader is a dictator. However, many groups and job situations may also have autocratic leaders. We sometimes call such leaders "bossy" people.

An example of an autocratic leader might be Jeff, the president of his class at North High School. Jeff knows that his ideas for the upcoming class party are good. He begins by setting up the committees and appointing each member to a committee. He then tells each committee exactly what he wants done. Jeff wants this party to be the best ever, and he will make sure it is. He leaves no room for other students' ideas or suggestions.

At the other extreme is the *laissez faire* leader. This person makes no decisions, but simply presents all relevant information to the members and allows them to initiate all action and to make all decisions. The laissez faire leader will not structure the organization, but after presenting the needed information, will fade into the background to a "do nothing" position. You could even argue that laissez faire leaders don't lead. They simply sit back and offer no suggestions or advice or help.

Doug is an example of a laissez faire leader. He is president of his youth group at church. He began the last meeting by asking the group if they wanted to invite a speaker to their next meeting. At that point, the group took over the discussion. Doug did not take part in the discussion until the group had decided to have a speaker. At that point, Doug said, "Good! If there is no other business, the meeting is dismissed."

But not all laissez faire leaders are "do nothing" leaders. Many are keenly aware of the happenings within the group, and influence the group in ways more than the members realize. This laissez faire leadership style might consist of recognizing or encouraging members who the leader knows will make the motion or suggestions he wants. Some groups can function well with this type of leadership.

The *democratic* leader combines the direction and guidance given by the autocratic leader, with the individual freedom of expression and choice provided by the laissez faire leader. The democratic leader develops goals for the group cooperatively and actively seeks input from members. Members are free to disagree or to get the group goals changed. But the leader will also assert his own goals for the group. Ultimately, the majority rules.

Denise is president of the student senate at Central High School. At their last meeting, she handed out an agenda of the topics to be discussed. The first topic was an all-school party. She asked for suggestions and listed all of them on the board. The group discussed each idea and finally decided on a plan. This led to plans for committees to carry out the suggestions. Denise asked for volunteers for each of the committees, suggesting that each committee select a chairman. Denise then went on to the next point on the agenda.

In a democratic organization, the leader allows members to decide their own policies and gives them the freedom to act on their own. The leader tries to treat each individual with respect and allows for maximum distribution of responsibility. As much as possible, decisions are made as a group. The leader offers suggestions, advice, and guidance. He/she serves mainly to maintain structure and initiate action. The democratic leader is the decision-maker only when the group cannot arrive at a decision themselves. Because of its size, America is not a democracy in the truest sense of the word. Our form of government is better called a republic, because we elect representatives to act on our behalf. However, at the small group level, democracy can be very effective.

To clarify the differences among autocratic, democratic and laissez faire leadership, imagine that you are an architect working under three bosses. Boss A insists that you do everything exactly as he wishes. Boss B assigns you jobs to do, but allows you the freedom to decide how you will accomplish the jobs. Boss C gives you the plans and tells you to build the building the way you feel is best. Which boss would you rather work for? Which boss is an autocratic leader? If you chose Boss A, you selected the autocratic leader.

Are there situations where autocratic leadership is sometimes necessary? What about leadership in the army or in the prison system? Generally, these two situations involve autocratic leadership. Is autocratic leadership the best type of leadership for these special cases? How well would these situations work with a laissez faire leader? What might happen if democratic leadership were used in the army and the prison system?

LEADERSHIP DEVELOPMENT ACTIVITY

MOCK CLASS ELECTION

You are about to participate in a mock class election. Your instructor will provide you with some specific directions about how to participate in this instructional activity. The goal for this activity is to help you identify and react to definitions of leadership advocated by four of your classmates who will be candidates running for office in the mock class election. The mock class election is designed to structure a safe, interpersonal situation in which you can apply and practice what you have learned about the definitions of leadership that different people advocate.

DIRECTIONS FOR MOCK CLASS ELECTION

1. Your instructor will divide the class into groups.

2. Get together with the other persons in your group and move your chairs into a circle. Try to leave some space between your group and the other groups.

3. Your instructor will assign to your group (or your group can request) one of the following definitions of leadership:

   —Leadership as personality
   —Leadership as a form of persuasion
   —Leadership as a power relation
   —Leadership as initiating action and maintaining structure

4. When your group has received a definition of leadership, spend a few moments talking about what your definition means. You may want to refer back to the definitions of leadership. Also talk about the type of campaign speech that might be given by a candidate advocating the definition of leadership that your group has been assigned.

5. When your group has discussed the definition and the speech, decide which person from your group will be your group's candidate in the mock class election. Also, decide on someone to give a nomination speech for your candidate.

6. Next, help the candidate and the nominator each write a brief "campaign" speech to be delivered before the entire class. Be sure that both speeches reflect the definition of leadership your group has been assigned. The following questions will help you to structure the speeches you write:

   Nomination Speech
     (1) Who is your candidate?
     (2) What is special about your candidate?
     (3) Why should people listen to your candidate?
     (4) What do you think of your candidate?

   Campaign Speech
     (1) Why are you a candidate?
     (2) What will you do if elected?
     (3) What experience have you had as a leader?
     (4) Why should people vote for you?

7. Notify your instructor when both speeches have been written. When all groups have completed their speeches, your instructor will assemble the class as a whole and outline the directions for the mock class election.

8. In the mock class election, each candidate and nominator will deliver a speech to the class. Immediately after each candidate and nominator have delivered the speeches, the class should write down the definition of leadership being advocated by the candidate-nominator team. When all candidate-nominator teams

9

have spoken, the class will vote to see which candidate-nominator team was most convincing. Ballots should be counted and the winner identified.

9. Following the identification of the winner, you will be asked to discuss each pair of speakers. At this time, each team will reveal the definition of leadership they represented. You will be asked to describe the techniques they used to influence the group, the elements of their speeches that contributed to their definition of leadership and the overall effectiveness of their speeches.

THINKING BACK

Think about the four qualities of a leader which were discusssed at the beginning of this chapter. How many of those qualities of a leader do you possess? Do you use them to influence your friends? Do. you influence people in a positive and constructive way? Think about some of the people who are leaders in your organizations at school, at church, or in the community. What makes them leaders? Why do you listen to them? How do they influence you?

Think about the speeches given during the mock election. If you were running for an elected office, what definition of leadership would you exhibit in a speech? Would you try to win the election on your personality alone? How persuasive could you be in a speech? How well could you influence your friends? How well could you influence a group of people you don't know?

Which method of leadership do you feel would work best for you? Why? What things do you need to consider as you choose your own method of leadership? Would you use a different method of leadership if you were president of your class than if you were a coach of a little league club? How might the methods vary if you were a manager of a department store, captain of the basketball team, head cheerleader, or president of the French club? What determines the type of leadership needed for a given organization?

ADDITIONAL ACTIVITIES

1. Write your own definition of leadership. According to that definition, are you a leader? Select another person from the class and discuss your definitions.

2. Identify a family, school, job or social situation where there is potential for you to improve your leadership skills. Write a one-page statement describing the situation and your feelings and reactions to the situation. Include a personal goal for this area of your life.

3. Select one leader in our country today. Listen to this person speaking to a group. How does he/she attempt to influence the listeners? What method of leadership is exhibited in the speech? If possible, listen to this person speak to different groups. Does his/her way of

speaking change? Are the methods used to influence the same from group to group or do they vary?

4. Prepare a brief inventory of your own special talents and abilities which might be related to your leadership abilities. Good leaders recognize their own special talents and use them as a part of their effort to lead. If you can speak well, you might stress speeches in your role as leader. If you are a good actor, you might become a dramatic leader. If you are good in art, you might stress posters in your campaign. What are the strengths, talents or abilities which you could use as a leader?

5. Identify a strong leader in school or in local politics. What are that person's strong talents or abilities? Does he/she seem to be very intelligent? Does the person speak or act well? Is he/she effective in dealing with people?

Chapter 2

OUTCOMES OF LEADERSHIP EDUCATION

OBJECTIVES

After finishing this chapter, you should be able to:

1. List at least five benefits of leadership training.
2. List at least five skills of leadership which can be developed.
3. Write a definition of citizenship and describe your responsibilities of citizenship.
4. Describe at least three levels of citizenship.
5. Recognize the benefits and skills of leadership in a leader of your community.
6. Write your own goals of leadership.

Have you ever heard the old cliche that "leaders are born, not made?" Many people use this phrase to argue that leadership training is not an important area of study.

Some individuals may be born with tendencies or characteristics of temperament which relate to their ability to function in leadership capacities in our society. At the same time, you know some people who seem to have many talents and abilities which should make them leaders, but they just cannot seem to use them constructively. Similarly, you know individuals who could function much better if they could just sharpen their basic communication skills a little. You probably also know someone who has given a speech to a group in a nervous, insecure fashion because he or she just did not prepare for the presentation or had not ever spoken before a group before. And, have you ever gone to a meeting and watched activities which were chaotic because of a total lack of organization by the leader or leaders?

Maybe leaders are born, but there are many leadership skills that can be taught. Many individuals can benefit from a systematic leadership education program regardless of how many natural talents they seem to have for leadership.

OUTCOMES OF LEADERSHIP EDUCATION

What does the future hold for you? Have you organized your thinking to the point that you have a basic idea as to your plans for the future? Many people do not. As you read this book, we hope that you will do some serious thinking about your future and what you plan to do with it. Regardless of the careers or personal relationships you choose to pursue, several common elements are present for most students. First, you will probably be working with people. Second, in some part of your personal or career life, you will probably be working in an organization. Third, you will probably become involved in civic or political activities and assume citizenship responsibilities.

Working with people, within organizations or as an ordinary citizen, you should try to maximize your potential by expanding your abilities. Leadership education can facilitate your leadership development. The outcomes of leadership education place you in a better position to take your basic leadership skills and develop these skills to the maximum possible.

PERSONAL DEVELOPMENT

One of the primary benefits of leadership education is personal development. Pause for a few minutes and reflect on your personal abilities. How would you rate your personal abilities? What are your strengths, your weaknesses? What aspects of your personal development do you think are in need of further development? Together, let's examine some of the areas of personal development that you might want to improve and illustrate how leadership education can be used to your benefit.

One of the first aspects of our development which can be enhanced by leadership education is self-esteem. By self-esteem, we mean how you feel about yourself, your self-confidence, self worth, and general well being. Involvement in a leadership education program and in a group can help your self-esteem grow because your successes generate rewards and reinforcement. Carrying out leadership tasks such as speaking to a large group, conducting a meeting of an important committee or getting elected to office, leads to growth in self-esteem.

Through this involvement, you will gain rewards or reinforcement. The reinforcement may come in the form of personal satisfaction. Personal satisfaction is a positive inner feeling that comes from knowing that you have helped someone or that you have completed a task. Similar to personal satisfaction is respect. Respect comes when people recognize that someone has done a good job or has demonstrated strong leadership and responsibility. This respect, combined with the satisfaction of knowing you helped someone else, results in self-respect. Self-confidence naturally follows. The three work very closely together. As you develop more self-confidence, you are more comfortable taking the leadership role. With more leadership opportunities, you have a greater chance to demonstrate your ability and to help others. This brings about more respect, self- respect, and personal satisfaction. All of these add up to a strong sense of security in yourself, your abilities, your job, and the position you hold as a leader. As a direct benefit of leadership education, your self-esteem has grown. Your personal development is greater.

A second area where leadership education can help the individual's personal development is in the area of communication skills. A direct benefit of a leadership education program can be the development of the ability to communicate more effectively with people. Have you ever spoken in front of a group? Many individuals are unable to speak in public and thus are unable to communicate their ideas to others. They may lack both the skill and the confidence, but to begin with, they need communication skills. Leadership courses and group activities can help you improve your communication skills. The best way to overcome the fear of speaking in public is to learn the necessary skills and then to gain experience in public speaking. Leadership development activities allow you to develop those speaking skills.

There are many other areas of communication to be developed in addition to public speaking. Listening, non-verbal skills, giving directions, directing a discussion, and writing are just a few. Many of them require practice to develop a high level of skill. Leadership education can serve as a catalyst in developing personal communication skills.

A third area in which leadership education can benefit personal development is the ability to get along with people. The reasons a person is not successful in a business position or in group leadership is often due to inability to get along with people. Leadership education can assist you in developing the ability to get along with people. You will learn specific interpersonal skills which will be valuable in a variety of social interactions. Conducting committee meetings, assisting in carrying out the activities of the group, working side by side with someone on a project, dealing with interpersonal conflicts of members — these are all types of leadership education activities which can help you develop skills in working with people.

A fourth area in which leadership education benefits the individual is in preparation to help others. As your skills and qualities as a leader develop, you will become aware of the many areas of service available to you in school, church, and community, as well as in the state and country. These skills will help you in helping others when you have the chance to serve as leader or member of civic, school or church organizations. Within a group, there are many opportunities to assist individuals who have personal problems or to assist individuals who are experiencing interpersonal conflicts in the group. You can also assist individuals who have special talents and who want to develop those talents in the group.

Some of the personal rewards and benefits of leadership education are more tangible. Your involvement in leadership education may lead to scholarships for college. This same involvement may also be influential in getting a job. When the abilities of candidates for scholarships or jobs are comparable, their backgrounds in civic, church, or school organizations are reviewed. Candidates who demonstrate leadership and responsibility are given preference. You might also get additional benefits in the form of promotion at work or a better paying job. Thus, the benefits of leadership education may be lifelong.

ORGANIZATION BENEFITS

Personal benefits occur as a result of the demonstration of certain skills of leadership. However, leadership education also produces benefits for the group or organization. Some of the leadership skills which benefit the organization, and which can be learned, are organization and planning skills. These group skills are needed when a leader plans meetings and organizes committees. Another related skill is initiating the action of the group. A good leader should not have to supervise all the work nor should he/she end up doing most of the work. Instead, the leader should appoint individuals and/or set up committees which are responsible for doing the work. With good, clear directions and goals, committees can do an effective job. In this way, a leader delegates authority. It is important for a good leader to learn how to initiate action and to communicate a charge or task to a committee so that the responsibility and the work are equally distributed in the group and so that the committee members understand clearly what they are supposed to do.

Another skill which a leader should possess and which benefits the organization is the ability to develop the goals of a group. A leader is able to involve the members of the group in this task. The leader is able to clarify the issues and the goals as the group discussion takes place. The leader also assists the group in the area of communication skills. This means that the leader can review and understand communication from a group and can communicate clearly to the group. The leader must also encourage more effective communication between the group members. A group leader must also help the group develop cohesiveness. This involves establishing an atmosphere within the group that encourages honesty, cooperation, and teamwork among the members. It occurs when the members respect each other and desire to work together to reach a common goal. The responsibility for establishing this atmosphere falls mainly on the leader of the group.

Parliamentary procedure is another skill which can be developed and which is of great benefit to groups and organizations. A leader conducts a meeting so that the group is efficient and effective. The leader is also able to adopt and adapt a style of leadership to fit the group and the situation. As discussed in Chapter One, the leader of a club at school uses an entirely different style of leadership than does the warden of a prison. Yet both are leaders. A leader must be able to understand the members, to adopt an appropriate style, and to adapt to the specific conditions and situations.

Finally, there are many times that you will find yourself in the position of group member rather than group leader. You will then be in a position to observe how the skills of the leader benefit the group or organization. You will also see how the leader is immensely dependent upon the skills of members to help the group function well and achieve its goals.

CITIZENSHIP BENEFITS

Citizenship is the responsibility a person has to society. There are many levels of citizenship, just as there are many levels of leadership. At the highest level of citizenship, citizens of the United States have the right and duty to participate in efforts to change, perfect or improve our ever evolving society. Citizens of the United States also have the privilege and responsibility of electing the President and congressmen. At the lower level of citizenship, we have the opportunity and responsibility to serve in a leadership capacity in situations at the neighborhood, local or state level. At the local level, the odds are great that we will be asked to serve as a chairperson or organizer for some activity. You might become a leader at a state youth organization meeting. At a more personal level, citizenship involves responsibility to family and friends. These units of leadership instruction will provide you with a wide range of leadership skills which you can use effectively in fulfilling your citizenship responsibilities and privileges.

You have a great potential for leadership in the fulfillment of citizenship responsibilities. You will have the opportunity to develop skills in planning and initiating action, developing a group goal, and cooperating in the attainment of that goal. You will have the opportunity to learn these skills from the standpoint of a leader and as a member of a group. You will have an opportunity to examine these skills and benefits and responsibilities to a greater extent in the group activity which follows. Finally, through related projects, you will have the opportunity to learn first-hand about the benefits and skills of leadership and citizenship.

PROJECT I. LEADERSHIP SURVEY

You are about to participate in a leadership survey. Your instructor will provide specific directions for this instructional activity. The goal of this activity is to provide an opportunity for you to discuss leadership and its related benefits with leaders in your community. This activity is designed to allow you to observe leadership in a real life setting.

DIRECTIONS FOR LEADERSHIP SURVEY

1. Your instructor will direct the class in the formation of a survey which will be used to interview some of the leaders of the community.
2. As a class, you will brainstorm possible questions which should be included on this leadership survey. The questions which will be used on the survey may be related to personal benefits, leadership skills, or the philosophy and goals of leadership.
3. As a class, decide on the criteria for evaluating which questions will be used on this survey. Also, as a group, decide on the types or categories of community leaders to interview.
4. Using the criteria developed in number three, compile an appropriate list of questions for the leadership survey.

5. Your instructor will now divide you into groups of two or three. Each group will select a civic, political, business, community, or religious leader to interview. Plan a time that you could schedule an interview with that person.

6. Schedule an interview with the leaders you selected. This can be done with a telephone call to the leader or to his or her secretary. Make sure to explain what the purpose of the interview is and how long the interview should take.

7. Decide on some related questions which might be useful to ask the leader because of his or her specific leadership position.

8. Prepare for the interview by getting the questions well in mind. Decide who will ask each question.

9. Conduct the interview. Be sure to dress well or appropriately for the interview.

10. After the interview, compile the information as soon as possible. Prepare a report to the class which will include your findings and interpretations of the person's leadership style and abilities.

11. Your instructor will now direct the class in compiling the information which was gathered by each of the groups. It should be possible for you to tally up responses to discover the most common answers given. You will be asked as a group to evaluate the findings and to discuss the overall effectiveness of the survey.

12. Write thank you letters to each interviewee.

PROJECT 2. THINKING BACK

The following list summarizes some of the most important personal outcomes or benefits of leadership resulting from the leadership education in the chapters which follow. Which ones are the most important to you? Why? Which are the least important to you? Why?

Preparation to help others
Personal satisfaction
Respect
Self-respect
Self-confidence
Sense of security
Scholarships
Better paying jobs
Job promotions

The list of leadership skills presented next summarizes some of the most important skills of leadership discussed in the remaining chapters. Which skills do you feel you have already mastered? Which skills represent weaknesses in your leadership capabilities? How effective are you as a group member?

Organizing and planning skills
Planning meetings

Organizing effective committees
Initiating the action of a group
Delegating authority
Developing the goals of a group
Communication skills
Fostering group cohesiveness
Parliamentary procedure
Adapting styles of leadership
Being an effective group member

At which of the following levels of citizenship are you prepared to take responsibility? What responsibilities do you possess already?

National
State
Community
School
Family and friends

ADDITIONAL ACTIVITIES

1. Think of some of your own personal goals of leadership. Make a list of as many as you can think of. Rewrite the list, dividing them into categories: personal (related to personality), skills, career, citizenship. Which list contains the most goals? The least? Select another person from the class and discuss your goals of leadership.

2. Which personal benefits of leadership training seem to be the most appealing to you? Perhaps you can add more to the list given in this chapter. Prepare a one-page statement describing the benefits you hope to possess following this leadership education class.

3. What is your philosophy of citizenship? How are we responsible to our country? To our state? To our community? To our family, friends, and school? Using magazines, markers, and poster board provided by the teacher, select one level of citizenship. Try to show how you view responsibility. Display the poster on the wall of the room. Be prepared to describe it to the class.

4. Think about the leader you interviewed as part of your group project. Prepare a profile of this person as a leader. What personal characteristics did you find outstanding? How could you develop some of these characteristics? In what ways does this leader influence the community? How do the skills of leadership affect his/her influence in the community?

Chapter 3

PERSONAL CHARACTERISTICS OF EFFECTIVE LEADERS

OBJECTIVES

After finishing this chapter, you should be able to:

1. Define seven personality traits of a leader.
2. Detect personality strengths and weaknesses in a leader, and suggest ways a leader should deal with a situation.
3. Identify and evaluate your own personaliy traits.

Susan has just completed her tenure as president of the Honor Society in her local school. At the awards banquet, Susan passed the gavel to the incoming president, while the Honor Society advisor, Mr. Melendez, spoke to the audience concerning the work the society has accomplished under Susan's leadership. As he concluded his comments, Mr. Melendez stressed that Susan possessed many qualities and characteristics of a good leader. Many of these characteristics were things that other students in the audience knew about and had observed during Susan's presidency. Mr. Melendez spoke of self-confidence, assertiveness, empathy, and responsibility.

PERSONAL CHARACTERISTICS

There are many qualities and characteristics which combine to produce a person who is an effective leader such as Susan in the above example. In the following sections, seven of those characteristics will be discussed. As you read these comments, please keep in mind that: (1) it is possible to be a good leader possessing all these characteristics and that (2) many of these characteristics can be developed. Which of these characteristics are strong points for you and which ones do you feel need improvement?

SELF-CONFIDENCE

Self-confidence or self-assurance has been found to be related to leadership. Leaders tend to possess more self-confidence than non-leaders. Leaders must be confident of their ability to handle the responsibilities and problems which accompany a leadership position. This is particularly important in the area of decision-making. Leaders make many decisions. Many times the decisions are needed quickly and there may not be time to do a great deal of thinking or to seek advice. A self-confident leader will remain calm and quickly evaluate the situation in order to make a decision "on the spot"

RISK TAKER

There will be times when the wrong decision will be made. When this occurs, the leader must be willing to admit a mistake and to start over. For this reason, an effective leader must also be a risk taker. Risk taking is closely related to self-confidence. A risk taker is exactly what the term describes - a person who is willing to take risks. Many times as a leader, you will be asked to "go out on a limb." Occasionally you will make decisions which are unpopular with the group. It is on these occasions that it is necessary to be a risk taker. Sometimes a group of people is not very receptive to something which is best for the group. A good leader should do what is best for the group, even if it means becoming unpopular. This requires a certain amount of courage as well.

WELL ADJUSTED

Effective leaders should be well-adjusted. Good leaders should not only be confident of their abilities and be willing to take risks, but they must also feel secure in themselves as persons. They need to have the maturity to be able to take criticism and advice. They must have the ability to admit mistakes rather than trying to cover them up or blaming others. They must have the security to accept others' ideas and opinions without feeling threatened. A well-adjusted leader will remain composed when too much is demanded or when too many decisions need to be made. The well-adjusted leader will not be afraid to delegate work to members of the group.

ASSERTIVE

Leaders also tend to be more assertive than non-leaders. An assertive leader will take command of a group when the situation calls for it. This personality trait is very much influenced by composition of the group. Some groups prefer a leader who does not dominate them. In this case, the assertive leader needs to adjust his/her personality to be less aggressive and more democratic. The opposite way holds true as well. Some groups prefer a great deal of direction and control. Effective leaders are aware of the needs of a group and can adjust their own assertiveness to meet those needs.

RESPONSIBLE

Successful leaders are also responsible. They are reliable and can be counted on to do what they have promised to do. This is a very important personality trait for a leader to possess. A group depends on the leader to carry out certain responsibilities. When the leader fails in those responsibilities, the group not only becomes less effective, but the individuals begin to lose confidence in the leader. Many times it is difficult to regain that confidence. An effective leader must be consistently responsible and reliable.

EMPATHY

Leaders tend to possess more interpersonal sensitivity than non-leaders. Sensitive leaders see the members of the groups as individuals with feelings and goals. Thus, they are not only aware of what the individual members are doing, but how they are feeling. One form of interpersonal sensitivity is empathy. Empathy is not only an awareness of feelings, but also an understanding of feelings in others. To a certain extent, an empathetic leader experiences the feelings of the members of the group. The qualities of interpersonal sensitivity and empathy are very important in the development of group cohesiveness.

EXTROVERTED

Leaders tend to be more extroverted than non-leaders. An extroverted person is more sociable, more talkative, more outgoing, and friendlier than an introverted person. Although extroversion generally seems to be an asset, it is possible for a leader to be too extroverted. There are times when it is necessary to be less outgoing. It is possible for a leader to talk too much and to create a negative reaction in the group. In order to be an effective leader, a person must be sensitive to the leadership situation and to adjust his/her leadership behavior to the characteristics and demands of the situation.

These seven personality traits are not meant to define the personality of the successful leader. Rather, the personality traits discussed must be considered in relation to a particular leadership situation. A personality trait can be an asset in one situation but a hindrance in a different situation. The successful leader is able to see how his or her personality is interacting with the situation and adjust as necessary.

LEADERSHIP DEVELOPMENT ACTIVITY

The following activity is designed to help you become more aware of your own personal style of leadership and to become more sensitive to the personal characteristics of others. The activity is called Leadership Development Case Studies and involves discussion of how the personal characteristics of the leader interact with the situation.

DIRECTIONS FOR LEADERSHIP DEVELOPMENT CASE STUDIES

1. Break into several small groups of four to six each. Elect a discussion leader in each group.
2. Each group is assigned one of the following four case studies.
3. Read each case study, discuss it, and answer the following four questions:

    a. What is the true problem?

    b. What are the important facts to be considered in the problem?

    c. What are several possible solutions?

    d. Which solution does your group recommend? Why?

4. When all groups have finished discussing the case study, each group should describe its case study to the total group. Give your answers to the four questions listed above.

LEADERSHIP DEVELOPMENT CASE 1

Dave Brody is a junior at Rodgers High School. Last October, he was elected to the office of vice president of his class. As vice president, he works with five other class officers, including the class president, Jim Forbes.

Having attended a state officers' training conference, Dave feels he is highly qualified for the office of vice president. He presents a good appearance, thinks well, and works hard. He has a pleasant personality and always gets along well with his friends.

Dave is also ambitious and wants to get ahead fast. Last October, he had hoped to be elected president of his class. He is now disappointed with his job as vice president because he feels it has little potential for his own future development.

After a state leadership workshop, Dave thinks about his office as vice president. He thinks the other class officers are unqualified for office and lack drive and ambition. He feels that Jim Forbes is a mediocre individual who was just lucky in being elected president of the class.

After much thought, Dave decides on a plan. He will avoid work on class activities except those involving the whole school. He will speak as often as possible before other groups of students. This tactic will give him the exposure and speaking experience he needs to become the student body president next year.

LEADERSHIP DEVELOPMENT CASE 2

Jill Becker has always been a natural leader. In school, she has frequently given advice and direction to her friends and classmates. About a year ago, Jill suddenly realized she could get her friends to do almost anything she wanted. Since then she has become more assertive.

Jill is the president of the French Club at Mariner High School. This is her third month in office and she has learned about duties quickly. Jill has now started giving directions to the other club members, but it seems they are not doing what Jill says, though she knows her directions are right.

LEADERSHIP DEVELOPMENT CASE 3

Mike Dunnigan has always been very neat and meticulous about himself as well as his work. He is a perfectionist. Mike has been a member of DECA (Distributive Education Clubs of America) for two years now. He has advanced from chapter president to regional vice president of the state association. He is neat and all his correspondence is typed and free of erasures and corrections.

Judy, also a high school student like Mike, has been appointed parliamentarian and has been in office one month. She is in the process of completing a project for the state association and asks Mike to review the final project after it is completed. Mike reads the final project Judy has completed and sends her this letter:

Dear Judy,

The project is far short of what I expected a good state officer would ever turn out. You didn't follow any of my suggestions. We need a parliamentarian who can do a job right - not an idiot! Next time, maybe you will ask the other officers for input and then we won't waste time doing the project over.

LEADERSHIP DEVELOPMENT CASE 4

Ken McDonald has been elected to an office in his church state youth association and has been given the authority and responsibility of the office of state reporter. Ken attended the state officers' training conference and has been a state officer for six months. Recently, the state president had asked Ken to take over the duties of state historian in addition to his present duties as reporter.

Three months passed and Ken noticed that the state meeting was just ahead. He had planned to start on the state scrapbook two months ago, but he couldn't decide how to organize the scrapbook. Although he has reviewed state scrapbooks from past years, he does not feel he has enough information to lay out the scrapbook intelligently, so he has not done so. Various local meetings are taking place and Ken has already had requests to show the state scrapbook that he hasn't even started yet.

Ken, quite worried about his scrapbook problem, talks to Susan, the state secretary. Ken says, "I don't know why someone doesn't tell me what to put into this scrapbook and how to organize it. This scrapbook problem has me so shook up that my stomach hurts. The same thing happened this winter with the news articles. By the time I got the articles into a useable and interesting format, the deadline for articles for the magazine had already passed."

THINKING BACK

As you review this chapter, it is important that you recognize the qualities of good leadership in yourself and in others. An effective leader is likely to be self-confident, well-adjusted, risk taking, assertive, responsible, extroverted, and sensitive. An effective leader must be the right balance of those qualities. A good balance of these traits gives effective leaders the security to surround themselves with people who are smarter than they are without feeling threatened. This balance gives them the sensitivity to listen to other people, to help them realize their goals, and to support them as individuals. This balance also gives them the maturity to realize that their authority is granted to them because of their position, and this authority must be treated in a responsible manner. This balance of traits also gives leaders both the security and the maturity to realize that there probably is not one best way to do any single task. This realizaton will allow them to better recognize the efforts and accomplishments of other individuals. This balance of traits will occur when the leaders take the time to analyze the group in order to adjust their personal style of leadership and their personal characteristics. The balance requires the leader to be sensitive to the members of the group as individuals.

DEVELOPING YOUR OWN PERSONAL QUALITIES AND CHARACTERISITCS FOR LEADERSHIP

This chapter has given you some ideas and some methods for developing your own personal qualities and characteristics of leadership. If you try to keep these ideas and methods in mind, you can continue the process for many years as you continue to try to grow as a leader. It will take concentration, effort and energy, but it can pay off in high level adult success in your field. In this section, we will suggest some ways you can continue this process on your own.

First, seek out opportunities to serve as a leader. You can volunteer to chair committees. You can agree to be a candidate in an election. You can seek opportunities to give speeches. As your performance improves, you will get more and more opportunities.

Second, always be open to and/or seek out evaluation of your work. Sometimes you can ask an audience or committee members to give you feedback about what went right or wrong. They can give their feedback in writing or in response to a questionnaire. In any event, you should try hard to get such evaluative feedback.

Third, when you get evaluative feedback, resist defensiveness. Don't look at it and begin defending yourself. Assume that they are honestly telling you what is wrong and ways you can improve. Weak people are likely to turn defensive or to argue against the feedback. As you grow stronger, you can begin to use member or audience feedback to improve yourself.

Fourth, ask some really good adult leaders to evaluate your performace. If they have become highly successful leaders, they will know how you can work to improve your leadership skills. Ask them to come and observe you in action. Such feedback should be really useful to you.

Fifth, take courses and/or training in leadership, communications, public speaking, teaching and/or supervision wherever you can find such training. There are many short courses of this type, and they can provide the guidance, direction and motivation you need to produce real growth in your leadership characteristics.

Sixth, set goals for yourself of the specific behaviors and characristics you want to work on. Put it in writing and keep track of what you are trying to accomplish. If it is written, you will be more likely to pursue it.

Seventh, seek out books, articles and checklists focusing on leadership characteristics which you might use. There are now many such publications on the market, and they can give you a lot of good ideas for personal development of leadership skills and personal characteristics.

Eighth, sit down periodically and evaluate yourself according to the goals you have set and using the feedback you have been able to get after your leadership and speaking experiences. Try to be objective and consider all the evidence dispassionately. Then revise and plan your goals for the future.

ADDITIONAL ACTIVITIES

1. You are the leader of a large group consisting of sixty members. Your group has recently decided to undertake an environmental cleanup project. In deciding the specific aspects of this project, you find that members have very different ideas concerning what the project should involve. You have recently decided that your group lacks direction and is unable to develop a unified course of action. What do you as leader plan to do about this situation? Consider how assertiveness and interpersonal sensitivity on your part influence or could influence the situation. Thus far you have not tried to dominate the group's planning. At the same time, you have not been sensitive to group members' opinions because your group is so large. With this as background information concerning the leadership situation, answer the following questions.

   a. Identify the true problem.
   b. What are the important facts to be considered in this problem?
   c. List several possible solutions.
   d. Which solution would you recommend as leader?
   e. How would you react to the solution you recommeded in question (d) if you were a member instead of the leader?
   f. What are the advantages and disadvantages of a leader adjusting to the demands of the situation?

2. The following items describe the personality traits of a leader. Read each item and check the response which best describes how you would most likely act if you were the leader of the group: always, frequently, occasionally, seldom or never.

If I were leader of a group . . .

	Always	Frequently	Occasionally	Seldom	Never
1. I would allow members total freedom in their work.	___	___	___	___	___
2. I would find time to listen to group members.	___	___	___	___	___
3. I would be willing to make changes when they were necessary.	___	___	___	___	___
4. I would be willing to take a stand on an issue I thought was important.	___	___	___	___	___
5. I would make sure I finished each task I began.	___	___	___	___	___
6. I would be friendly and approachable.	___	___	___	___	___
7. I would be willing to accept the responsibility for the actions of the group.	___	___	___	___	___
8. I would speak out when I had a good idea.	___	___	___	___	___
9. I would seek to understand the other members of the group.	___	___	___	___	___
10. I would treat all members of the group as equals.	___	___	___	___	___
11. I would be willing to change my style of leadership to fit the group.	___	___	___	___	___
12. I would refrain from talking when other members were contributing to the discussion.	___	___	___	___	___
13. I would keep the group members working as a team.	___	___	___	___	___
14. I would try out my ideas on the group.	___	___	___	___	___
15. I would share my authority with other group members.	___	___	___	___	___

	Always	Frequently	Occasionally	Seldom	Never
16. I would trust the group members to use good judgement.	—	—	—	—	—
17. I would do those things I had promised to do.	—	—	—	—	—
18. I would act as a real leader of the group.	—	—	—	—	—
19. I would get group approval before proceeding in important matters.	—	—	—	—	—
20. I would seek what was best for the group over what was best for myself.					

Review each item above and examine each response that you gave. Of the characteristics discussed in this chapter, which ones seem to be your stongest traits? Which seem to be your weakest? Take a few minutes to formulate a goal for the development of some personality traits of leadership in your life. In what ways can this charactersitic be developed?

3. Which of the characteristics from this chapter do you feel are the most important traits of an effective leader? How do these traits interact with each other? Develop a character profile of what you feel would be an ideal leader. Share that profile with a friend. Together, develop a profile which uses ideas from the two other profiles. Be prepared to share your final profile with the entire class.

4. Observe some of the leaders in your school, community, state, or country. List some leadership charactersitics evidenced in them. Do you observe any qualities which are not discussed in this chapter? Add those qualities to your list.

Chapter 4

SKILLS OF A GROUP LEADER

OBJECTIVES

Upon completion of this chapter, you should be able to:

1. List and describe the four basic functions of a leader.
2. Name at least six skills of a group leader.
3. Describe how to lead a small group discussion.
4. Demonstrate the creative problem solving process in a group situation.
5. Distinguish constructive humor from destructive humor.
6. Explain three ways to evaluate a leader's effectiveness.

In the last chapter, the personal characteristics of a leader were discussed. Though these traits can be developed to a certain extent, they are also natural characteristics. In this chapter, you will learn about the skills which can be learned by almost anyone. These are the types of skills that can be perfected through study and practice. As you read through this chapter, observe those skills which you have mastered already. Observe as well those skills with which you have had little previous experience. Those are the skills which you will need to practice.

BASIC FUNCTIONS OF A LEADER

A good leader performs basic functions in a group. In a democratic society, these are indispensable leadership behaviors.

One function performed by a good leader is to promote free interaction among members. All members are given a chance to participate and express their views.

If a group is to be cohesive and happy, the members of the group must feel free to express their opinions, ideas, criticism, and to influence the goals and activities of the group. This cannot occur if the leader or fellow members are apathetic, critical, or unreceptive to new ideas. In order to achieve this freedom of speech and influence, the leader must refrain from excesses of harsh criticism and must encourage the members of the group to be open as well.

Consider the following case study. Susan is the president of the science club. At a science club meeting, a heated discussion developed over a proposed club trip. One part of the membership wished to tour a local industry while another faction wanted to attend an athletic event. As president, Susan directed the discussion between the two factions. She skillfully allowed members from each group to express their views. Once the total group voted for one trip, each party had been given equal opportunity to express their views. Susan had promoted freedom of expression of divergent views.

Another function of a leader involves fairness. A good leader must strive to be fair in all deliberations, decisions, and actions. Group members can very easily lose confidence in a leader who shows favoritism or is unfair in treatment of members in the group. A leader must treat each person equally and consider each person as decisions are made relative to the group.

Using the example of the science club president, Susan, we can see that leadership was displayed and fairness was stressed. Susan did not dictate or impose her views on the membership. The group was allowed to make a democratic decision.

Decision making skills are an important function of a leader. An effective leader must be able to make decisions based on the views of the majority of the group. Sometimes these decisions may be contrary to the leader's own preferred choice of action. The leader must be able to respond positively and to encourage a positive attitude in other members of the group as well. Such actions will help to enhance the cohesiveness of the group and will assure productive decision making.

Frustration levels rise in a group when a leader is reluctant to make decisions. An effective leader displays decisiveness while guiding an organization. Susan moved quickly to accept the votes of the club, then began the process of organizing the trip. Susan did not delay in carrying out the group's desires.

Another function of an effective leader is to protect the rights of individual group members and the rights of minority subgroups of the total membership. Individuals and subgroups should be encouraged to assert their own views and to try to persuade the majority of their merits. The leader must assist individuals and minority subgroups in this process.

Susan's effective leadership not only carried out the vote of the majority, but also allowed the minority to express their views, thereby protecting their rights. Even when the minority is only one member, that member has the right to be heard.

The final function of the leader is to help all group members to achieve their personal goals. This function can best be accomplished as the group makes decisions together and follows through as a team. This is probably the most difficult function to learn and to accomplish. It requires a great deal of interpersonal sensitivity.

SKILLS OF A GROUP LEADER

The functions of a leader require the possession of a variety of skills. The effective leader must be skillful in the following activities:

A. Decision making
B. Oral and written communication
C. Parliamentary procedure
D. Public relations
E. Discussion in large and small groups
F. Creative problem solving
G. Using questions to develop group understanding
H. Using humor effectively

DECISION MAKING

Decision making skills are important because a leader is often required to make decisions for the group or to assist the group in making decisions. The leader must be able to evaluate the situation as well as the goals, needs, and characteristics of group members in making decisions. Not only must the leader be a good decision maker, he/she must be able to teach the group members this skill as well. The development of this skill will promote greater effectiveness in the group as the members gain the ability to make wise decisions and move quickly.

COMMUNICATION

In any group, it is necessary for the leader to be able to communicate well with members. Success in dealing with people may depend a great deal upon being able to communicate goals and directions to group members and on understanding communications from group members. Oral and written communication are very important. A leader should develop skills in both areas and in transmitting and receiving. In order to participate in group meetings, he/she must be able to understand what the group is saying or thinking and what it wants. This may involve verbal communication with one person or with many people. Many opportunities will arise which will require communication in speaking, listening, writing, and reading. The communication skills will be discussed further in a later chapter.

PARLIAMENTARY PROCEDURE

A critical leadership skill is parliamentary procedure. The leader must understand the formal rules for conducting a meeting. A productive meeting will be well-organized and orderly. The effective leader helps the group learn how to use parliamentary procedures in solving problems, achieving goals, and meeting the needs of individual members. (For a detailed discussion of parliamentary skills, see Chapter 10.)

PUBLIC RELATIONS

A leader should also possess public relations skills. Public relations skills include keeping the people of the community informed, gaining community support, and attracting the interest of prospective members. The use of these skills is called publicity. Good publicity requires the leader to be honest, accurate, and consistent. Good publicity also requires much work on the part of the leader. He/she must be able to survey all possibilities for publicity, make an effort to meet people, learn to remember and use names, and learn how to make proper introductions. A leader who possesses public relations skills will help strengthen the group by obtaining much needed support from outside the group.

DISCUSSION LEADER

The leader will often be called upon to lead discussions in large and small groups. Leading a group discussion usually serves the purpose of clarifying ideas or developing goals and plans for some activities. Skill in leading discussions requires much practice and usually develops slowly in prospective leaders.

The following are some guidelines for leading a small group discussion:

A. Prepare for the discussion - plan well.
B. Organize the group or call the meeting.
C. Introduce the topic, goals or problem.
D. Keep the discussion on the topic.
E. Keep the discussion moving forward.
F. Give all a chance to contribute.
G. Keep the discussion from becoming too heated.
H. Stimulate discussion by asking questions.
I. Summarize the discussion at the end of the meeting.
J. Announce the next topic for discussion.

QUESTIONS TO STIMULATE DISCUSSION

Another skill required of a leader is question asking. The skillful use of questions will help promote a thinking group. Questions enable the leader to encourage group involvement in a discussion. Questions also encourage an atmosphere of group decision making. Questions are used in the process of discussion or formal meetings to advance the goals of a group.

HUMOR

Many effective leaders also use humor effectively. A good sense of humor on the part of the leader will help the group to relax and become more efficient and effective in its work. Some guidelines for using humor effectively are:

A. If you cannot use humor effectively, do not use it at all.
B. Use a humorous situation only for a legitimate purpose.
C. If you want to use a funny story, write it out as it should be spoken and rehearse its delivery.
D. Use humor that makes a point. The humor should be related to your topic.
E. Select humorous anecdotes with care. Avoid vulgar content or any theme that might offend others.

CREATIVE PROBLEM SOLVING

Sometimes the leader must also be able to lead groups in the discovery of unique solutions to problems. This process is called creative problem solving (Feldhusen and Treffinger, 1980). Several steps of creative problem solving are presented next.

BRAINSTORMING PROBLEMS

Brainstorming can be used to identify problems for a group. The directions for brainstorming are to list as many problems as possible during a given amount of time. The participants are also instructed that all members are encouraged to participate. Farfetched ideas are also encouraged because they may trigger more practical ideas. The combining of several ideas or the building upon other people's ideas is acceptable as well. There should be no evaluation or criticism of ideas. Everyone should feel free to offer ideas. When the brainstorming of problems ends, the group goes to work evaluating the seriousness of the problems listed. They can reduce the list until finally they have identified the one most serious problem for immediate action. That becomes the problem they will work on in subsequent steps.

CLARIFYING THE PROBLEM

During this step, the group expands and clarifies the problem. This is accomplished by listing illustrations and causes of the problem. The group is also asked to describe further problems caused by the problem.

STATEMENT OF THE PROBLEM

Now the group is asked to state the problem as clearly and precisely as possible in the form of a question. For example, the most critical problem for our school might be a lack of school spirit. The question developed during this step would be: "How can we encourage more school spirit in our student body?"

BRAINSTORMING SOLUTIONS

Now the group participates in several techniques to develop new and unusual solutions to the problem. Generally, they use brainstorming to identify a large quantity of solutions to the problem. The solutions may involve what can be done to solve the problem or how things can be changed to improve the problem situation. Participants are encouraged to see the problem as a whole and as a product of its individual components.

EVALUATION AND SYNTHESIS OF SOLUTIONS

The participants now select the best solutions from their brainstorming of solutions. They are encouraged to combine several solutions or the parts of several solutions into one uniform solution to their problem. Once a final solution is developed, the participants are asked to evaluate the solution by looking back to the original problem. They are asked to observe how completely the problem has been solved as a whole.

IMPLEMENTATION

In the last step of creative problem solving, the participants must make plans to implement the solution they developed in the previous step. They are asked to consider who will be involved, what steps must be taken, what obstacles they will face, and how those obstacles will be overcome.

The process of creative problem solving is a useful tool for groups to learn. By following the model described here and outlined in the leadership development activity, your group can be more productive and creative in project activity.

EVALUATING LEADER EFFECTIVENESS

A good leader maintains effectiveness by securing evaluations of his/her performance as a leader. There are several ways evaluation can be obtained.

INFORMAL EVALUATION

One informal method of evaluation is for the leader to observe the group in action. How effectively and efficiently does the group function? Is the group accomplishing its goals? How do the members respond to me as their leader? This method calls for the leader to put aside biases and personal interests and to try to be objective in assessing the group.

A second method of evaluation is also rather informal. This is the discussion method of leader evaluation. The leader can ask the group for feedback regarding the group and the leader's effectiveness in the group. The leader should encourage openness and honesty when this method of evaluation is chosen. It is important to consider all comments that are made to avoid defensiveness. With this method and the first described above, the leader must make notes after the session to catch the main criticisms and suggestions.

A final method of informal leadership evaluation is use of a leader developed questionnaire. This is an instrument prepared by the leader and administered to the group. It may involve such broad questions as the following:

1. Has the leader helped us clarify our goals?
2. Are meetings well planned?
3. Does the leader use parliamentary procedures effectively?
4. Is the leader respected by group members?

The leader who uses this method will select questions which focus on critical areas of concern. Usually, responses are presented anonymously.

FORMAL EVALUATIONS

A more formal type of evaluation is the Leadership Behavior Description Questionnaire (LBDQ) (Stogdill, 1974). This is a systematic method for reviewing leadership skills by asking group members to evaluate the leader according to a specified list of skills. The list includes the critical abilities which a good leader should have. It is one of the most widely used such instruments. It provides excellent feedback for improving leadership behavior. The Leadership Behavior Description Questionnaire is designed to subject important areas and aspects of leadership behavior to scientific analysis.

LEADERSHIP DEVELOPMENT ACTIVITY

Your teacher will ask you to divide into groups of four to six for a creative problem solving activity. Once in your groups, you will be instructed to select a secretary who will be responsible for writing all of the responses given by the group.

Step 1. Brainstorming Problems

Rules. There should be no criticism during the brainstorming. Farfetched ideas are encouraged because they may trigger more practical ideas. Quantity of ideas is the goal. Building on other people's ideas is acceptable. All group members should participate. Here is the problem.
What are the most serious problems students face as a result of the energy crisis?
Brainstorm for seven minutes.

Step 2. Evaluating the Problems

Now the group should spend about ten minutes evaluating the problems brainstormed. The goal is to reduce the list to three and then to one most serious problem.

Step 3. Clarifying the Problem

In this step, the group will try to make sure that they all agree on the problem. They should ask such questions as the following:
A. What are illustrations of the problem?
B. What are the causes of the problem?
C. What are further problems caused by the problem?

Step 4. Statement of the Problem

In this step, the group attempts to state the problem as a question. Using the information from Step 3, they should write a question, possibly beginning with "How can we . . .?" and finish with a statement of the desired solution.

Step 5. Brainstorming Solutions

In Step 5, the group turns back to brainstorming to solve the problem. What are possible solutions to the problem? What could be done? What could be changed? Again, there should be a secretary to record all ideas, and the rules of brainstorming should be followed. At this stage, it is important for the group to think of as many new and unusual solutions as possible. Think about all of the parts of the problem and how each of those parts might be solved.

Step 6. Evaluation and Synthesis of Solutions

In this stage of creative problem solving, the group endeavors to pick out the best solutions from Step 5 and create a composite solution. This is both an evaluative and synthesizing process. The best elements of solution from Step 5 are identified and combined into an integrated solution.

Step 7. Implementation

In Step 7, the group plans for implementation or application of their solution by answering these questions:

How will we implement our solution?
1. Who will do what?
2. What are the steps that must be followed?
3. What obstacles must be watched for?
4. How will those obstacles be overcome?

When the creative problem solving process has been completed, the group should discuss its strengths and weaknesses in the creative problem solving process. If the group is quite young (e.g., first to third graders), a simplified creative problem solving process should be used (Feldhusen and Moore, 1979).

THINKING BACK

Think back about the four functions of the leader. Which function do you feel is the most important to the group? What are some ways that these functions might be developed? How accepting are you of others' opinions? What problems may result if a leader is not fair? What is the basis for good decision making? How can a leader know what the personal goals of the followers are?

Think back about the nine skills of a leader which were discussed in the chapter. Which skills do you feel confident of? Which skills will require more practice? Why do you feel that this area of communication is so important? How can you practice your skills of leadership?

ADDITIONAL ACTIVITIES

1. One method of producing unusual solutions to a problem involves forced relationships. This technique uses common objects to develop solutions. The group is given a problem and one or more objects. They are then instructed to use the objects to arrive at a solution to the problem. Your problem: How can we improve our schoool? Develop a solution using a tennis ball, a leaf, and an envelope. Use one or several at a time.

2. Another technique used to produce unusual solution is called synectics. Synectics involves taking those things which are familiar and making them unfamiliar and conversely, taking those things which are unfamiliar and making them familiar. Two types of synectics are fantasy and personal. Fantasy synectics require the problem solver to develop a solution that is totally

fantasy, while personal synectics ask the problem solver to put himself into the problem. Your problem: How can we improve our school?

A. Develop a solution which is totally fantasy. The more far out, the better. It can be as crazy or ridiculous as you wish. For example, how would they create a perfect school on Fantasy Island or on Gilligan's Island?

B. Develop a solution by answering this question: If I were a school, how would I want to be improved so that I might better serve the students, faculty, and administration?

3. Using the solutions developed in activities one and two, develop a practical answer to the question: How could we improve the school? List the steps that would be necessary for you to implement the solutions to the problem. With the help of your teacher and principal, begin to implement your solution.

4. With paper and pencil, listen to a public speaker giving a speech. Write a description of attempts to use humor in the speech. What techniques did the speaker use to bring humor into the speech? How effective was the sense of humor? Which techniques would you choose in a speech?

5. Imagine that your club is having a membership drive, and you have been chosen to be the publicity chairman.

A. List the steps you would take to publicize the membership drive and your club.

B. Make a list of all of the people you would need to contact during this time.

C. Prepare one poster publicizing your club.

D. Share your work with two or three other people in the group. Evaluate your effectiveness as a public relations person. What are the criteria for evaluation?

REFERENCES

Feldhusen, J. F. and Treffinger, D. J. *Creative thinking and problem solving in gifted education.* Dubuque: Kendall/Hunt, 1980.

Feldhusen, J. F. and Moore, D. L. A simplified creative problem solving model. *Journal for the Education of the Gifted*, 1979, 3, 61-72

Stogdill, R. M. *Handbook of leadership.* New York: Free Press, 1974.

Chapter 5

COMMUNICATION SKILLS FOR LEADERS

OBJECTIVES

After finishing this chapter, you should be able to:

1. Identify the various types of communication.
2. List the components of clear communication.
3. Present a speech to a group.
4. Demonstrate the communication skills of listening and giving directions.
5. Discuss methods for effective communication in the following areas: giving directions, listening, interpreting nonverbal cues, understanding people, making conversation and introductions, writing letters, and giving speeches.

Communication can most easily be defined as "the sending and receiving of messages." Probably no one skill or personal characteristic is as important to the success of a group leader or group member as the skill of good communication. Good communication is necessary for a group to be cohesive, effective and efficient. A good leader must be able to express ideas and explain plans in a way that everyone in the group will understand. Each member must be able to listen carefully and to follow directions in addition to expressing ideas in a clear, concise and precise manner. Whenever people are working together, communication problems arise. Often, the sender of the message assumes that the receiver understands more than he/she actually does. Many times the receiver of the message fails to ask for clarification of the message being sent. This will result in misinterpretation of the message, which may lead to more problems later. Sometimes, the receiver of the message will misunderstand nonverbal cues and thus misunderstand the message. These sound like simple problems, but they represent a breakdown in the communication process.

COMMUNICATION SKILLS

Good communication requires skill and practice. It involves the leader and every member of the group. It occurs through spoken words and written words, as well as the nonverbal cues of facial expressions, gestures, and other body movements. Communication takes place each time a word is spoken, written, heard or read.

Lack of communication is the cause of many problems and misunderstandings in a group. Poor communication may result from unclear directions, ineffective listening, conflicting nonverbal communications, and lack of understanding of human nature. Perhaps the most serious communication problem is the inability to express ideas clearly, orally or in writing.

Each of these problems will be discussed in this chapter. Keep in mind that the whole communication process is very complex. You are responsible for the "sending" of your message. You have a very limited control of how it will be received by other people. Your responsibility is to make your message as clear, concise and precise as possible.

GIVING DIRECTIONS

Mary Baker is the president of her junior class at Haywood High School. A class meeting has been called to discuss the progress made so far on the junior/senior banquet. Mary asked for a report from each committee chairperson, but each said that they had not done anything because they were not sure what to do. Mary became very upset with them and said, "Do I have to do this all myself? I told you what to do last week when we had the meeting. Can't you follow directions?" Upon further discussion, Mary learned that the meeting had lasted longer than she had planned and she had given the instructions hurriedly, assuming they were understood. There was no time left for questions.

Giving instructions is a part of every person's life. Think how many times you explain how to find a specific location like your house or a store. Think, too, of how many times you explain how to do something like homework or a craft of some type. The process of giving directions is a part of your everyday life, and it is not reserved for the leader of a group. You may not be the leader, but you could very easily be a committee chairperson. Here are some guidelines to consider as you give directions:

Begin with a brief overview of what you are going to try to do. Give your listeners an organizer so that they can see clearly in a general way what you plan to describe to them in detail. In a large group, limit your directions to the people involved. Some directions are not meant for the entire group. When this occurs, both the speaker and the listeners can very easily be distracted by people who are not interested in what is being said. On these occasions, it is best to move out of the large group into a smaller group.

Wait for the attention of each person who needs to hear the directions. This is a technique which is necessaery for any size group. Before proceeding, pause until everyone is silent and has focused attention on you. This will help eliminate repetition due to inattentiveness. But repetition may still be desirable to assure effective communication.

Try to go step-by-step. Try to refrain from putting in details where they do not belong. If you suddenly remember that you have forgotten to say something, save it until the instructions are finished, rather than "throwing it in" where it does not belong.

Keep the directions as short as possible. Because you need to be as concise as possible, try to exclude any details that are not necessary to the instructions. The shorter the directions, the greater the chance they will be understood and remembered.

If possible, ask the listeners to repeat the directions to you. This will help them remember the directions and will also help test their understanding of the directions.

Be very careful not to leave out significant details or concepts. This may mean that you provide context clues during the explanation. You may launch into an explanation of a committee task but forget to explain that your group advisor specifically requested that this task be done. Be sure to consider what fundamental details must be given.

Ask if there are any questions. Allow time for the listeners to clarify any details that may be unclear. This should help them understand the instructions as a whole. Above all, be patient during a question period even if the same question is asked several times.

Finally, summarize. Restate the plan or instructions briefly. Emphasize major points which may be forgotten or misunderstood. Help the listener to achieve closure.

These ideas do not ensure that you will never have problems when you give directions, but they should help eliminate many problems which may arise. Your goal is to be understood clearly.

LISTENING SKILLS

Speaking is only half of the communication process. Listening is just as vital as talking. Many times, people "tune-out" a speaker. They may be thinking about what the speaker has just said or how they will reply to the speaker. Some people have also become passive listeners. Overexposure to TV dulls our attentiveness. Some people also have hearing difficulties and thus never really get the message, or they miss significant parts of it. Sometimes, people do not listen because their minds are on something totally unrelated to the speaker's message. They may be thinking of what they are going to do later or what they did earlier. Perhaps they are thinking about a problem which they have. Regardless of the reason for their inattentiveness, they are missing what the speaker is saying. Attitude may also influence listening. People sometimes have difficulty listening to someone with whom they disagree.

Listening is a common courtesy which everyone ought to exhibit. Because good communication requires respect for and consideration of the other person, it is important that you concentrate on listening. Listening is a skill which needs to be practiced. The following methods can be used to improve your listening skills.

Look at the person who is speaking. This will help you concentrate on what he/she is saying. Acknowledge that you are listening by nodding your head or occasionally interjecting an "I agree" or "That is true," etc. This will let the speaker know you are listening and will help keep you actively involved. Keep alert to what the other person is saying. This may require quite a bit of mental discipline, but don't let your mind wander. Ask questions if possible. Questions help clarify what has been said and indicate your interest in what the speaker has said. Reflect on what the person has said by summarizing or putting what the person has said into words. This can be done verbally to the presenter, "What you're saying is . . . ," or mentally at another time. Try to be sincerely interested in the subject. This may prove the most difficult task of listening. It, too, requires mental discipline as well as respect for the other person.

Think about how easy it is to ask someone to repeat what they have said. Notice how evident this is in your classes and at home. Sometimes, we expect to have the information repeated so there is no reason to listen the first time. Think about the classic example of a man reading a paper while his wife talks to him. She can say anything and he will probably agree. Most of us have not trained ourselves to listen properly. Sometimes we miss the information completely. Yet listening is a good way to learn new information. How good a listener are you?

NONVERBAL COMMUNICATION

You constantly communicate with other people. Some of the messages you send are in the form of nonverbal communication or body language. Body language may take the form of a facial gesture such as a smile, frown, a raised eyebrow, or a wrinkled brow. Body language can also be expressed in gestures of the hands, arms, or shoulders. Sometimes the way a person walks or stands may communicate a message to someone else. Oftentimes, body language is the only way you can understand what a person is thinking.

Because she was thinking as she listened, Terri usually had a frown on her face. The members of her group thought that she disapproved of what they were saying. Bob can never look at someone when he talks to them. Instead, his eyes usually look at the floor. This causes people not to trust him. When Jane talks, she uses very extreme hand gestures. Her friends think they are funny and occasionally mimic her. Whenever Alice talks to someone, she has a smile on her face. This helps people feel more comfortable and at ease around her. As John listens, he raises his eyebrows. This helps people know that he is thinking about what they are saying.

It is important to learn to read body language. A smile can indicate friendliness or acceptance or happiness. Sometimes a smile can indicate cynicism as well. A frown may display anger or disagreement or confusion. Much can also be learned by observing the position of the eyebrows and jaws, as well as the movement of the eyes. When you speak, it is important to notice other body language such as yawning, slouching, and general inattentiveness. The message indicated here is that you have spoken long enough and your audience is bored.

Sometimes these nonverbal messages conflict with the words which are spoken. When these two aspects of communication conflict, it is a good idea to ask for clarification. The presenter may not be aware of the body signs he or she is projecting. A well framed question may be necessary to clarify the situation.

While it is important to be able to read nonverbal messages, you must never assume that you know exactly what someone is thinking or feeling when they haven't expressed it in words. Body language only provides cues for added understanding. It is easy to misunderstand nonverbal messages. Many times, people are not aware of the message their body is transmitting. Thus, you should express your lack of understanding and ask for further clarification.

UNDERSTANDING OTHERS

A major part of communication includes relating to other people. This relating requires that you understand something about their experiences, needs, and problems. As you speak to a group or an individual, consider their interests and experiences. In doing this, you can relate your information to what they already know. This is beneficial because it helps them grasp something which may be new to them. It also helps develop a relationship between you and your audience as they see that you are interested in them.

Communication also involves understanding the problems of other people. Sometimes this requires you to overlook certain negative comments that are made as well as some negative nonverbal messages. There will be times when you must give someone the benefit of the doubt, realizing that the person is "just having a bad day." As a member of a group, you must allow other members to make mistakes. Hopefully, they will allow you to make mistakes as well. Criticism and complaints create a negative atmosphere which does not promote good communication.

Personal communication can be very difficult. It does not thrive on prejudices, stereotypes, or insensitivity. In order to communicate effectively, you must consider the whole person and attempt to relate to the person as a unique individual.

Sally is a good illustration of effective personal communication. When Jim failed to show up for the car wash, she phoned him and asked if anything was wrong. When he explained that he had been having some problems at school, she asked if there was anything she could do to help. He replied that he just didn't feel up to coming to the car wash. Sally explained that they could use him and would like him to be there, but that she understood. This encouraged Jim and helped strengthen their relationship.

EFFECTIVE COMMUNICATION

Effective communication is a very complex process. It requires a variety of skills. In addition to the skills of giving directions, listening, interpreting nonverbal cues, and understanding people, there are many other oral and written communication skills. Some of these skills involve quite formal modes of communication such as public speaking or business letters. Many other communication skills are less formal, such as a personal letter, a discussion, or a conversation. Here are ten general rules to consider as you communicate with others. They are applicable to both formal and informal communication, as well as both oral and written communication.

1. Be accurate. Violating this rule can be very dangerous. Try to make sure that your facts are true and up-to-date.
2. Be brief. Try to say as much as you can in the least amount of time.
3. Be clear. Though you want to be brief, make sure that you say exactly what you mean. Avoid complex word combinations, phrases that have double meanings, or subject material that might be misunderstood.
4. Don't try to impress your audience. Be authentic and sincere. People do not respond positively to boasting and arrogance.
5. Consider your audience. Select vocabulary, illustrations, and material which your audience can understand and relate to.
6. Think and organize before you write or speak. Try not to ramble.
7. Make your message interesting. Say something worthwhile and use interesting stories and illustrations. Practice your delivery.
8. Don't leave out essential facts. Remember the five W's (Who, What, When, Where, and Why) and How.
9. Don't just relate it, illustrate it! Use actual objects, models, movies, photos and illustrations whenever you can.

There are many specific situations which will require you to communicate effectively. The rest of the chapter will consider several of them.

THE CONVERSATION

A conversation is an informal exchange of ideas. This is probably the most common type of communication. There are many opportunities for conversation. Before beginning a conversation, consider the other person's interests. Observe any books, magazines, or other items which might provide some common ground for a conversation. For example, if a person is carrying a runner's magazine, you might begin the conversation by asking if he or she is interested in jogging.

Be considerate and sensitive of the other people. Be alert to how busy they are. They may not appreciate being interrupted. Try to notice how they are responding as well. If the answers are a simple "yes" or a nod, they may be responding only to be polite. In this case, you might not want to continue the conversation.

If the person is a stranger, avoid questions of a personal nature such as "How old are you?" or "Where do you live?" Also, try to avoid excessively controversial topics. You can easily end a conversation if you are too opinionated.

Conversation with people you already know will not be as difficult. Because you are acquainted, you have a common base to begin your conversation. In conversations with both strangers and acquaintances, be sensitive about the amount of time you spend speaking. It is easy to talk too much and dominate the conversation. This is inconsiderate and insensitive. It is equally bad to remain silent. Look for opportunities to contribute your share to the conversation. Don't allow one person to control the discussion.

MAKING INTRODUCTIONS

There will be many times that you are called upon to make introductions. A good introduction, whether formal or informal, should provide the names of the people being introduced and some information about them. "Mr. Black, this is Bob Smith. Bob is the vice-president of our club. Bob, this is Mr. Black, our new faculty advisor."

As a general rule, younger people should be introduced to older people. "Mr. Smith, this is John Adams. John, this is Mr. Smith." Also, men should be presented to women, regardless of age. "Mary Smith, this is Mr. Adams. Mr. Adams, this is Mary Smith."

In a group, a special guest or visitor should be introduced to the officers of the club or organization. A visitor or guest should be introduced to several people at a time. "Mr. Jones, these are our officers: Mary Smith, Roberta Andrews, Fred Clark, and Alan Wagner. This is our speaker, Mr. Jones."

There will also be times when you will introduce yourself. Offer your right hand, identify yourself, and give a brief explanation about yourself. "Hi, I'm John Brown. I'm president of the FFA Chapter in Cedar Hill." Usually, the other person will offer his or her name and you can begin a conversation.

You will also be called upon to make formal introductions. Formal introductions take place when you introduce a speaker to the audience. These introductions should include the name of the speaker, a brief explanation of the speaker's background, and a description of accomplishments of the speaker. You should also take this time to officially welcome the speaker to the meeting.

WRITING LETTERS

Letter writing is a frequent duty of the group leader. It is important that you practice your letter writing skills. Letters may be informal, like the letters you write to your friends and family. The letters which will be discussed in this chapter, however, are the formal letters you might write in connection with your group responsibilities.

Letters may be written for a variety of reasons. Because they are less expensive than a telephone call, they are a good way to communicate for group business. Your group may be inviting a speaker to address a meeting. They may be requesting information which the group needs to finish a project. They may need to provide a speaker with more information or confirmation of a speaker date. They may want to thank a speaker for a presentation to the group. Letters also provide a written record of what has been communicated, in case there are any questions later.

Because you want to make a good impression on the reader, the appearance of the letter is very important. If possible, the letter should be typed or written neatly in blue or black ink. The letter should be re-read several times to check for errors in spelling and grammar. The overall appearance of the letter should be neat. Use plain, white paper with even margins at the top, bottom and sides. Of course, if your group has letterhead, you will use it. Never use notebook or lined paper.

Try to fold the paper so that it opens ready to read. Make as few folds as possible in order to fit the envelope. For formal letters, a business envelope is appropriate. Place your return address on the upper left corner of the envelope. The address should include the title of the person receiving the letter and the complete address.

A good formal letter should include eight main parts:

1. Date letter is written.
2. Name and complete address of the person to whom the letter is written.
3. Salutation: e.g., "Dear Ms. Black:"
4. Body of the letter. This should include the purpose of the letter, facts or requests for information organized into paragraphs, and a concluding statement. "Thank you" is usually in order.
5. Closing phrase: "Sincerely yours,"
6. Your name. If the letter is typed, your signature should be in ink with your name typed below the signature.
7. Your title or office, e.g., President, FFA.
8. Your address. If you have business stationary with a letterhead, your address is already provided. If you are using plain white paper, your address should appear above the date.

Figure 1 gives an illustration of a bad letter and Figure 2 gives an illustration of a well composed and well written letter.

Figure 1

June 24, 1983

Mr. James Gray
United Industries
1212 North Broadway
Kansas City, Missouri 56788

Dear Mr. Gray:

Our group is studying leadership in executive positions. We appreciate your coming and speaking to us on that subject. When would be a good time for you to speak?

Thank you very much.

Sincerely

Mike Jones
President, Junior Achievement

233 White Lane
Lee Summit, Kansas 56777

Figure 2

233 White Lane
Lee Summit, Kansas 56777

June 24, 1981

Mr. James Gray
United Industries
1212 North Broadway
Kansas City, Missouri 56788

Dear Mr. Gray:

I am the president of Junior Achievement in Lee Summit. Our group is currently studying the leadership skills and responsibilities of a business executive. We would like to invite you to speak to our group on the topic of your choice. Our club normally meets the first Tuesday evening of every month, but we are willing to set up a special meeting to accommodate your schedule.

Thank you very much for your time, and I will look forward to hearing from you.

Cordially yours,

Mike Jones
President, Junior Achievement

PRESENTING A SPEECH OR REPORT

Presenting a speech can be frightening for those who are shy in front of groups or for those who have little experience in speaking. The important part of speaking is the preparation. Good preparation for the speech can help to boost confidence. Some guidelines for speech preparation are given in the following sections.

Choose Your Topic Carefully

The general purpose or goal of a speech might be: 1) to inform or instruct, 2) to entertain, 3) to persuade (to secure some form of action) or 4) to impress people. The same purposes apply to writing. A topic that you already know something about or a topic about which there is plenty of information is best. It is important to begin planning by considering your audience and the occasion. How many people will be there? Will both sexes be present? What are their interests and attitudes? What do they already know about the topic? What is the purpose of the meeting and your speech? How is the talk related to the total program? How much audience participation is expected? All of these questions will help determine what will be presented and how it will be presented.

Organize the Speech

In organizing your speech, begin by searching for current, up-to-date information. This may take you to the library for books and periodicals. Collect the information on cards, noting the sources. Sift through all you have collected and select the information you will use, then begin writing the speech as an outline. The introduction should gain the attention of the audience and define specific terms. The conclusion should tie the material together into a central theme, providing a simple summary. The main body of the speech should develop and illustrate the ideas. When you have finished the outline, begin trying to give the speech. Practice to a mirror or with a friend and make notes of errors or problems to be corrected.

Make Use of Neat, Readable Visual Aids

Good visual aids can be an asset to any speech. Learn how to use a chalkboard and overhead projector. Other good visual aids are slides, filmstrips, films, charts, and graphs. These help keep the attention of the audience and clarify difficult concepts. Added emphasis is given to information which is both heard and seen.

Speak at Normal Rate and Sufficiently Loud and Clear

The delivery of the speech is very important. The words must be spoken at a good normal rate of speed, not too slow, not too fast. This is very difficult when you are nervous. Experience will help develop this skill. The speech must be loud enough for everyone to hear. If the crowd is quite large, you will have to watch your audience carefully for signs of difficulty in hearing. The words must also be enunciated clearly and precisely. This becomes easier as you learn to speak at an appropriate rate. The delivery of your speech will be more effective and interesting if you learn to vary your speed and volume as well as word emphasis.

Watch Your Posture

Maintain good erect posture while speaking. Remember, the podium, lectern, or table are meant to aid you in giving your speech, not to support you or to hide you. Do not cling to these pieces of furniture or drape yourself over them. Try to assume a comfortable position which is relaxing to you without being too informal.

Practice Giving Your Speech

Practice the delivery of your speech. Become as familiar with the outline as possible. Experiment with the speed and volume of your delivery. Sometimes practicing in front of a mirror is useful. Develop some effective gestures. Try to refrain from making distracting motions. Practice will help you feel more comfortable and relaxed when you are giving your speech. This will help control the speed of the speech. Some speakers memorize their outline as a security measure to free them from notes while speaking.

Get Feedback

A good way to make progress is to get feedback each time you speak. You can give out questionnaires to the audience, asking for anonymous evaluations, or you can call on selected friends to give you detailed feedback. Such evaluations can be very helpful in correcting problems in presentation.

Finish on Time

Make sure you know exactly how long you are to speak. Try to stay within the allotted time. This can be accomplished by limiting how much you plan to say. Try to leave the audience with a favorable impression. Choose an interesting illustration or story which will give a strong, crisp ending to your speech.

These are only a few suggestions for effective public speaking. Composure in front of an audience will only come through practice and preparation. If you follow the steps outlined above, you will begin to see improvement in your public speaking.

THINKING BACK

Think about communication. What is it? What are the types of communication? What promotes good communication? What brings about a lack of communication?

Are you a good communicator? What are the components of clear communication? Can you give and accept constructive criticism or feedback? Do you listen carefully when others are speaking? Do you ask questions when you don't understand something another person has said? How well can you give directions?

How well can you read nonverbal cues? How observant are you of body language? Are you aware of the nonverbal cues which you send? What do you do when nonverbal messages conflict with verbal messages?

How well do you understand others? Are you sensitive to the needs and problems of individuals in your group? Can you make allowances for personal differences? Do you tend to think in terms of stereotypes?

How well can you begin a conversation with a stranger? Can you keep the conversation going? How do you handle controversial topics when they are discussed in a conversation?

When was the last time that you introduced yourself to someone? Did you make that introduction correctly? How well do you introduce other people? What are the suggestions to keep in mind when you make introductions?

Can you write a formal business letter? Why is it important to proofread letters before you send them? What are some of the times when you would write a letter for your organization or club?

How do you go about selecting a topic to use for a speech? What should you consider as you select that topic? What are the steps you should use in preparing and making that speech?

Communication is a very complex process. Yet it takes place every day in almost every situation you face. The skills of communication have been discussed briefly in this chapter. If you remember the ideas for good communication presented in this chapter, and try to practice the skills you have learned, you will begin to improve your communication skills.

ADDITIONAL ACTIVITIES

1. Tape record your next group meeting. At the next class session, play back the tape and write a one page description of the effectiveness of the communication that occurred. Answer the following questions. Were there moments of confusion? How were they dealt with? What was your contribution to the meeting? Had you wanted to say something but refrained from doing so? What are the strengths of the group in the area of communication? What are some of the weaknesses of the group in the area of communication?

2. Prepare a short demonstration for the class, explaining how to do something. Try to have enough materials available for everyone in the class to participate in the activity. Evaluate how well they followed your directions.

3. Using a mirror, practice nonverbal communication. Select several attitudes or emotions and try to portray them nonverbally. Present one or two of them in class to see how well your classmates can interpret them. Try to use as many parts of your body as you can.

4. Review the sections on conversation, introductions, and letter writing. Within the next two weeks, begin a conversation with someone that you do not know, write a business letter, and make an introduction. Be prepared to evaluate each situation and discuss it in class.

5. Review the steps involved in preparing a speech or report. Prepare a five to seven minute informative speech for the class. Remember to practice your speech.

Chapter 6

LEADERSHIP SKILLS FOR GROUP MEMBERS

OBJECTIVES

After finishing this chapter, you should be able to:

1. List and explain three reasons for joining a group.
2. Compare the personal qualities of a group member and the skills of a group member.
3. Explain the characteristics that are necessary for a group to be successful.
4. Recognize the role each member plays in your group.
5. Evaluate the leader and members of a group in a case study.

INTRODUCTION

This chapter differs from the previous chapters in that it focuses on the members of the group rather than the leader. An effective group will only have one or two leaders, but it must have a number of members. There is a very good chance that you are either a member of a group now or that you will be a member in the future. This chapter is designed to help you learn those characteristics and skills necessary to be a good group member. Remember, a group leader can only be as successful as the group members he/she leads. Unless the members are doing their job, the leader cannot do his/her job. A well-run group depends on the cooperative work of the leader and the members. As you read this chapter and participate in the activities, think of the groups of which you are a member. Think about what you are doing as a member and what the other members are doing.

WHY DO WE JOIN GROUPS?

Most of you belong to at least one group. Some of you belong to a number of different groups. Why did you join each group? What does each group offer you? There are four basic reasons an individual joins a group: security, new experiences, recognition, and shared interests and goals. Most of us feel the need for acceptance, stability and a secure position in life. Being a member of a group allows you to be assured of a "niche" or place in society in which to seek companionship, entertainment, and service. All of these lead to a feeling of security. A good group should be able to provide this security.

Paul Smith is an example of an individual seeking security. He plans to attend a university next year and has decided to pledge a fraternity. He feels that because of the size of the university, a fraternity will help him meet people and will provide many opportunities to enjoy himself. He has talked to several fraternity members and appreciates the public service they do as well. His next step will be to visit several houses during rush activities to decide which fraternity to join.

Many people, like Paul, also join groups for the new experiences the group offers. A group provides opportunities for meeting new people and having new responsibilities. In addition, groups offer a medium for exchanging ideas, playing new roles, and developing new skills. Most groups carry on a variety of social and service activities, and those activities can provide members with a diversity of experiences.

Beth Jones joined 4-H this fall for exactly the reasons which were just discussed. She knew that 4-H provided an opportunity to meet new people throughout the state as well as to learn how to do certain projects. She hopes to get involved in the state leadership as well. These experiences can be a great source of learning as well as pleasure.

Some group members enjoy the recognition of being a member of a certain group. Everyone enjoys prestige, influence and attention. Though we may hate to admit it, this motivation is important. Usually, this recognition is achieved because of the public service or the status of a group.

Bob Adams joined a group which raises funds for the local children's home. He had the opportunity to present those funds to the telethon chairman on TV. Bob was glad to be able to help and he had to admit that it was fun to be on TV. He also enjoyed all of the comments his friends made about him. He achieved a great deal of recognition and status through the activity.

The last reason an individual joins a group is shared interests and goals. It is enjoyable to be around people who have similar interests and goals. We can share ideas with them, knowing that they will be well-received and accepted. Because of the shared interests of the groups, there can be a greater sense of unity. The shared goals make it possible for an individual member to accomplish some purposes which he or she values or needs. The sense of unity can be very helpful during those times when we feel a need to share problems with someone else. It is easier to share a problem with someone who understands us. A group can foster this understanding. But above all, a group makes it possible for us to achieve both individual and group goals.

Bobbi Clark joined her church youth group because the members were very easy to talk to. She found that the other individuals felt the way she did about many different issues. She was glad that there were some differences as well. She really appreciated being able to talk to Sue when she was having problems at school. She also found that by working with the church youth group, she could accomplish some of her own goals which she could not achieve alone.

UNIQUE CONTRIBUTIONS OF GROUP MEMBERS

Each member of the group has his/her own personal reason for joining the group. In the same way, because each individual is unique and brings a distinctive contribution to the group, each member brings unique interests, drives, and motivations. These motives help draw the member to the club and help keep interest in the club alive. Each member also contributes expectations and aspirations. These characteristics help challenge growth in the individual, as well as other members of the group. Each individual also brings definite values, attitudes, habits, feelings, and beliefs. These characteristics can help the members learn from each other and continually grow in the area of personal interaction. Each member also contributes premonitions, frustrations, inhibitions, and fears. These characteristics will help promote an attitude of caution in the group, thus providing a balance for those who might be too eager. These characteristics cause the group to consider the problems that might occur and to evaluate what the group is doing. Finally, each member brings to the group unique and individual adjustment patterns for past failures. Each of us learns from our mistakes. Each member of the group can contribute something from past experience to assure group success in the future.

PERSONAL QUALITIES OF A GROUP MEMBER

In addition to the unique contributions made to the group, it is desirable that each member possess some personal qualities. A member should be dedicated to the group and to its goals and objectives. This requires the member to be loyal and supportive of the group. A group member should also display a willingness to work for the organization and to do that work thoroughly. This is closely related to the personal qualities of energy and enthusiasm. All three suggest a desire to bring about progress and growth in the group.

A group member must also be willing to cooperate and to compromise and to seek what is best for the group as a whole. A good group member should be honest in dealings with others, both in the group and out of the group. A group member should be reliable as well. It is important that each member can be counted on to do assigned tasks. Part of this reliability involves punctuality. Members should try to be on time at meetings and related group activities. Finally, it is important that a group member be friendly and sociable. Outgoing, warm members are an asset to any organization. They improve interaction and openness among members. A part of being friendly includes the ability to be sensitive to the needs of other members in the group. But not everyone will possess all of these personal qualities. Good group members, however, should demonstrate most of them. They should also be in the process of developing the others as well. A group will not be effective if the members are not willing to work toward a common goal. Many times this involves dedication, willingness, and compromise, as well as all of the other qualities mentioned above. The ultimate goal of every member should be to make the group as successful as possible.

SKILLS OF A GROUP MEMBER

Not only should group members exhibit certain personal qualities, they should also possess certain membership skills. The first skill involves communication. Good group members must know how to say exactly what they mean. They must be able to organize and communicate their thoughts. They must also be able to listen and evaluate what has been said. Communication skills also include public speaking.

Group members must also possess certain social skills. Social skills include remembering names, knowing how to make introductions, and knowing proper etiquette for various occasions such as meetings, ceremonies, and banquets.

Another type of skill is a combination of social and communication skills: knowing how to persuade other people. Persuasion is the ability to sell an idea or to convince the other members of the group that your idea is good. Many times, the idea chosen by the group will depend on which member is the most persuasive. Group members who have creative ideas must be able to persuade the group to accept and develop their ideas.

The development of these skills requires experience and practice. As you work with people, you will learn how to interact with them successfully. Communication, social, and persuasion skills are basic abilities which you must acquire in order to become an effective group member. These skills were discussed in more detail in Chapter 5.

CASE STUDY

Bill James is a junior at Roosevelt High School. He is involved in many extra-curricular activities including basketball, student government, and the science club. Bill was elected to the student senate last year, but he is not an officer this year. Bill attends every meeting and tries to arrive on time. Bill stayed late several nights to help make the props for Harvest Happening, a fall party for all high school students. His booth, which featured health food treats, was successful and he was pleased when Jan Jewell, a student senate member, commended him at the next senate meeting. Bill hopes to be elected to an office next year. He feels that the position of president or vice-president might help him promote more school spirit and appreciation of the faculty. Bill thinks he has a good chance for the election because his classmates like him and he is often asked to help out on class and school projects. Bill is respected for his good sportsmanship on the basketball court and for the school spirit he displays at all school events.

RESPONSIBILITIES OF GROUP MEMBERS

We have now discussed the reasons people join groups, how each person contributes to the group, and the qualities and skills of a good group member. The next topic is the responsibilities of members. The responsibilities of group members fall into two categories: responsibilities to the group and responsibilities to the members.

One responsibility an individual has to the group involves committee work. A group member has the responsibility of working on committees and of accepting appointments made by the officers. A good group member seeks to be involved in a reasonable amount of appropriate committee activities. There are times, however, when a group member must also accept the responsibility for doing assigned tasks. In this case, the individual may be doing a job that would not have been chosen. It is important then that the job be done well even though the member's interest may have been low in the particular activity.

Another responsibility an individual has to the group involves making a contribution. It is important that the group be supported through participation in discussion and activities. A group member must be willing to take part in group activities, help the group make decisions, and state views and opinions. It is easy for some members to sit back and let others do the thinking and talking, but a good group member feels obligated to contribute.

A group member is also responsible to fellow members. He or she must not only be willing to present views, but also be willing to be quiet when someone else is presenting a position. Each individual must respect the right of other members to be heard, treated courteously, and to disagree. These are all closely related to the social skills mentioned earlier.

A group member must realize that to fail in a responsibility to a group member is to fail in responsibility to the group. Conversely, when an individual fails the group, he/she is also failing the individuals in that group.

WHAT IS A SUCCESSFUL GROUP?

With an understanding of effective group leadership and good group membership, it is now possible to describe the traits of a successful group. Success of a group can be described in three areas: task behaviors, social behaviors and membership attitudes and policies.

When a successful group is involved in a task or activity or project, several behaviors should be visible. These behaviors can best be described as a series of steps. The first behavior or step is giving suggestions or directions by the leader. The group will then give opinions, make evaluations and analyze and express feelings related to the task which is about to begin. This is the second step. The third step takes place when the leader gives more orientation about the subject, repeats or clarifies information about the subject, and confirms any comments that might have been made. After the project has been started, the members once again ask for more orientation, information, repetition, or confirmation. This fourth step allows them to learn if they really understand what they are doing, and if they are doing the project as their leader planned.

The fifth step takes place as the leader once again gives information relevant to the task. The next step occurs when the members ask the leader for opinions, evaluations, analysis and expression of feeling about the activity or project. Sometimes, they can also ask other members for evaluation. This is a very important step because our involvement in a group project may blind us to weaknesses in the group process. An objective opinion can be very beneficial. In the final step, the leader asks for suggestions and opinions about the activity. In this way, the leader can better understand how well group members have worked or not worked together and how his/her leadership ability or failures have affected group activities.

Social behaviors necessary for a successful group include those behaviors which raise the status, give help, or reward other members. Behaviors which build group cohesion and cooperation will help make a successful group. Examples of these social behaviors include compromising when the group is deadlocked, asking for help when the group is unable to complete a task, being honest but sensitive to the needs and feelings of other members, and stepping back occasionally in order to evaluate the situation.

Finally, groups are more likely to be successful when a new member feels warmly received. New members must feel that they are a part of the group. Membership policies are also important. Groups tend to be more successful when there is a clear distinction between members and non-members. Thus, it is important that there be a clear-cut definition of a member, with requirements outlined in the bylaws. In this way, members will have a greater sense of belonging. It is also important to involve senior members in the selection process when individual members leave and need to be replaced. In this way, older members are given more influence in the group.

GROUP ROLES

To understand a group, you must be able to identify the kind of contribution each member makes to it. No one performs the same function or "plays the same role" in a group all of the time. Most of us will be limited to a few functions or roles in a particular group. In another group, our roles may be quite different. Group roles can be defined in two broad categories: work roles and maintenance roles. Work roles involve those roles that are most obvious when an activity or project is in progress. They involve members in productive contributions to projects which are being carried on by the group. Maintenance roles involve those activities which sustain group activities or progress. They involve participation in discussion, making new members welcome, promoting the organization informally in the community, etc.

GROUP ACTIVITY

Figure 6-1 shows the roles people play in a group activity or meeting. On the next page is a case study taken from the minutes of a meeting of the Lincoln High School Student Senate. President Barb Adams is just starting the meeting. As you read through the minutes, notice those aspects of the group that make it successful. At the same time, take note of those aspects that could be improved. Look also for the roles which people are playing and try to characterize them according to the model presented in Figure 6-1.

Figure 6-1

Group Task Roles*

Work Roles	Maintenance Roles
1. Initiator: Proposing tasks, goals or actions: defining group problems; suggesting procedures.	1. Harmonizer: Attempting to reconcile disagreements; reducing tension; getting people to explore differences.
2. Informer: Offering facts; giving expression of feeling; giving an opinion.	2. Gate Keeper: Helping to keep communication channels open; facilitating the participation of others; suggesting procedures that permit sharing remarks.
3. Clarifier: Interpreting ideas or suggestions; defining terms; clarifying issues before group.	3. Consensus Tester: Asking to see if a group is nearing a decision; sending up a trial balloon to test a possible conclusion.
4. Summarizer: Pulling together related ideas; restating suggestions; offering a decision or conclusion for group to consider.	4. Encourager: Being friendly warm and responsive to others; indicating by facial expression or remark the acceptance of others' contributions.
5. Reality Tester: Making a critical analysis of an idea; testing an idea against some data trying to see if the idea would work.	5. Compromiser: When one's own idea or status is involved in a conflict, offering a compromise which yields status; admitting error.

*Adapted from "Understanding Your Group" Farmland Industries, Kansas City, Missouri.

CASE STUDY

President Barb Adams asked repeatedly for attention so the meeting could begin.

Mary Asher asked when the meeting would be over. She said she had to study for an English test.

Barb said it would end at 1:30.

Barb stated that the purpose of this meeting would be to decide on a theme for the spring senate program.

John Myers stated that he didn't feel we needed a spring program because we had a Valentine's Banquet.

Sherry Brown said she thought they needed to have one because they always have one.

John stated that if we did have one, he would not help.

Barb said that was OK. She then asked for suggestions for the theme.

Jim Wagner suggested a western theme.

Jerri Hawkins said that was a stupid idea because we had that two years ago.

Barb asked for other ideas.

Jane Smith suggested a 1950's theme.

Many members of the group felt that was a good idea.

Barb asked if everyone wanted that and most of the members raised their hands.

Barb stated that the theme would be the 1950's and set up five committees:

> Decorations: Jerri Hawkins, Chairperson
> Food: Jane Smith, Chairperson
> Entertainment: Jim Wagner, Chairperson
> Clean-up: Mary Asher, Chairperson
> Promotion: Carolyn Davis, Chairperson

Mary pointed out that Carolyn was absent because she was studying for the English test, so Barb appointed Andrea Wayne as chairperson.

Barb asked for volunteers for each committee, but no one volunteered. She appointed committees as follows:

> Decoration: Jill and Sarah
> Food: Elaine and Judy
> Clean-up: Mike and Ruth
> Promotion: Wayne and Brian
> Entertainment: Valerie and Doug

Barb instructed each group to plan for about fifteen minutes and report back to the group. Mary dismissed her group and left saying she did not have time. Barb met briefly with each group and clarified what they needed to consider. After fifteen minutes, she asked for a preliminary report from each chairperson.

Jim said that the entertainment committee had decided they did not like the 1950's theme and would prefer a Western night.

Barb stated that the decision had been made by her group and that they needed to keep it as it is. Jim left...

As a group, discuss this case study. Knowing what you know about parliamentary procedure, how well has this meeting been conducted? How do you feel about the leadership of this group? What is Barb doing well as a leader? Where could she improve? What problems exist with these members? What qualities and responsibilities are exhibited? Which qualities and responsibilities are lacking? How successful do you feel this group is?

THINKING BACK

Think about the groups you are now a member of. What benefits do you receive because you are a member? What were your reasons for joining? How do those reasons compare with the reasons which were discussed earlier in the chapter? Are there other reasons which were not discussed? Did you receive benefits which you did not consider? Were you planning on any benefits which did not occur?

Think about your unique talents and abilities. How have those talents and abilities been used in your group? Which talents and abilities are not being used in your group? Look over the section entitled "Unique Contributions of Group Members." Which of those contributions have you used in your group? Are there other contributions you have made to your group that were not discussed in the chapter?

Think about the personal qualities and skills of a group member. How do the qualities differ from the skills? How are they related? Which qualities and skills do you possess? Which are in the process of being developed? Which qualities and skills do you feel are the most important in working with a group?

What responsibilties do you have in the groups you have joined? How have you helped make each group more cohesive and successful? What could you do that would build more group cohesion? What could you do to make each group more successful? How cohesive and successful do you feel that the groups are?

ADDITIONAL ACTIVITIES

1. Look back at the group roles listed in Figure 6-1. Select five members of your group and decide which roles they play most often. Which other roles do they play? Now decide which role you play most often. How do you feel about that role? How could it be changed? Compare your discoveries and ideas with another member of the class.

2. Reread the minutes from the case study included in the group member activity. Using the class discussion and analysis, rewrite those minutes so that the group appears more successful and the members seem more responsible and cooperative. Change the role of Barb so that she is a better leader as well.

3. Do a brainstorming activity with a group of three or four other

students. List as many different responsibilities you have to a group as you can think of. Then list as many different contributions to a group that you can make.

Chapter 7
DEVELOPING GROUP GOALS

OBJECTIVES

Upon completion of this chapter, you should be able to:

1. Define what is meant by value, goal, objective and motivation.
2. Demonstrate the consensus-seeking process.
3. Develop a leadership goal for your life.
4. Describe the value underlying the goal you develop.
5. Outline the steps involved in attaining your goal.
6. Write one objective for the attainment of your goal, using the ABCD model.

INTRODUCTION

The success of a group is determined by many things. First, quality leadership is necessary for a group to function effectively. Second, the positive involvement of group members is important as well. Third, little can be accomplished without good communication between the members and the leader. And, fourth, the development of a set of goals is an important aspect of enhancing success of the group.

The discussion in this chapter concerns the development of group goals. Leaders and individuals who study leadership education function within the framework of a group. A leader must lead. This implies that some action is to take place. The action is implementation of the goals of the group being lead.

IMPORTANCE OF SETTING GOALS

Successful groups set goals. The major political parties establish platforms based on the political goals of their respective parties. In a similar manner, your organization and/or club will decide on its activities (or goals) for the year.

Leaders and individuals set personal goals. Every day we formulate a variety of goals for ourselves. The goals vary in their importance and in the amount of time we spend thinking about them. Your goals for the future in terms of career and family should require much more thought and planning than the plans which you have for this weekend or next summer. It is important that you learn to develop goals wisely so that efforts by the group or by yourself are not directed toward an end which is not satisfying or worthwhile.

GOAL PLANNING MODEL

The setting of goals either by groups or an individual should be carefully considered. A systematic approach can be a valuable aid in the process of setting goals. Figure 7-1 depicts a simple planning model that includes four components.

First, values of groups or individuals are clarified. Second, goal statements are formulated. Third, specific action objectives are developed. And, fourth, short and long term implementation plans are developed.

Values

Goals

Objectives

Short and Long
Term Plans

Figure 7-1: System for Developing Group Goals,
Objectives and Activities

VALUES

Before group members can clarify their values, the word value must be defined. A value can be defined as a consistent belief by an individual that an object or idea is desirable as a goal or action. This definition suggests that a value is the degree of importance that we place on any activity, object, or goal. For example, if you placed friendship high, friendship as a value would be very important to you.

Values can be clarified in at least four ways. First, you can become more aware of your own values and how they relate to your decisions. This requires self-examination on your part. You must take the time to think about your likes and dislikes. Which people, activities, and things in your life do you hold in the highest regard? How do those aspects of your life affect the way you think and act?

A second and very important step is for you to make your values consistent and decide which ones are most important to you. This step will determine the course of action you will take in many situations. For example, your values would be inconsistent (or in conflict with one another) if you considered good health important, but did nothing to bring about physical fitness. Eating unhealthy foods and failing to get proper exercise suggest that your value of good health is less important to you than the satisfaction you gain by eating junk food and not exercising.

A third way you can clarify your values is to become more aware of the differences between your values and the values of others. Most other people do not value the same things you do. This process makes you more aware of your own values as well.

Finally, a fourth way to clarify values is to learn to tolerate the differences that exist between your values and the values of others. This is a difficult task, but it can be accomplished by learning to discuss rather than argue and to share rather than to try to convince. Listening also helps you learn how to accept the values of others.

The use of this four step value clarification process will be more meaningful if you go through each step in the same way you would do a homework assignment. Write down your response to Step 1; then as noted in Step 2, decide which items are most important to you. Deciding which items are most important can be done by prioritizing the list of items. For Steps 3 and 4, compare your prioritized list with the list of your friends, parents, teachers, etc.

Clarifying Values of a Group

Like individuals, groups must clarify their values. Many groups have goals and purposes developed as a part of their group character. Yet, often these groups need to review their values to test the validity of the goals. As was discussed earlier, the goals and purposes of the group should be based on a set of values which are embraced by the majority of the group.

Group value clarification can be done by employing a three step procedure. First, divide the group into smaller subgroups. Each subgroup should brainstorm and develop a list of values perceived important to the subgroup. This list is then written on a chalkboard for examination by the other subgroups.

Second, each subgroup orally describes its list of values to the entire body. This allows for all subgroups to share the composite thinking of the group. Then, each subgroup uses the information from the other subgroups and reviews its own list of values. A second subgroup list of values is generated based on all the discussion thus far.

Third, the revised subgroup lists are again discussed as a whole group. The entire group then agrees upon the commonalities of the lists. These common elements provide the base list of values upon which the group develops its goals and purposes.

Group leaders are important to this group clarification process. Leaders must keep the subgroups focused on the task, provide input, and help the groups arrive at a set of values.

PRESENTING AND CLARIFYING GOALS

Once an individual or group has clarified values, the process of setting goals can begin. If a group already has a set of goals, it might be wise to examine the goals in light of the clarified values of the group.

Webster defines goal as "the end toward which effort is directed." The purpose of a goal is to specify or define an end. The goals of a group identify the targets toward which the group's activities are aimed. The goals of a group help determine which activities will be pursued by the group or the individuals in the group. In this way, the activities can be evaluated and put in a priority list in order to make the best use of the group's time and resources.

Group goals also help promote understanding and agreement within the group. This builds group cohesiveness. As people take part in planning and decision-making, they will feel more involved and motivated to help. This will be very important when help from individuals is required. Finally, goals serve to ensure that the needs of the group are met. For example, a relevant goal of a chess club would be to provide opportunities for its members to play in tournament chess games.

In summary, group goals provide a target for the group, a method of evaluating the activities of a group, a system to foster group cohesiveness and understanding, and a way to ensure that the individual needs of the members of a group will be met.

Setting Group Goals

There are five guidelines which should be followed when a group or individual sets up goals.

1. Provide Adequate Time. Don't allow the process of setting goals to be rushed. Remember the potential effectiveness of a group or individual depends largely on the goals which are set by them. Time must be given for incubation of ideas—thinking them through. This can best be accomplished away from group meetings and other people.

2. Explore Ideas, Interests, Values, and Needs of the Group Members. This can best be accomplished through the process of brainstorming, which will produce lists of ideas and suggestions. Do not allow evaluation or criticism during this stage. The key during this exploratory stage is to produce as many ideas as possible, to let people state their interests, values or needs without fear of evaluation.

3. Secure Consensus. During this step, evaluation of the ideas will take place. Ideas or goals which are inconsistent or contrary to the wishes of the majority of the group can be eliminated. The second part of this step involves group decision-making to select the most important goals. Care should be taken to limit the number of goals to a reasonable number which can be accomplished during a given period of time.

4. Formulate a Statement. Once goals have been chosen by a group, related goals can be combined to form other goals. For example, a service organization may produce objectives related to community service: city clean-up, charity benefits, and senior citizen visitation. These might all be combined under the general goal of "promote civic responsibility." The goals should next be combined to form a general goal statement for the group.

5. Ensure Common Understanding and Acceptance. After the goal statement has been formulated, it must be presented to the group again and discussed in order to bring about group understanding and

acceptance. If the goals are to be effective, each member of the group must thoroughly understand and accept them.

Setting Individual Goals

For individual goal setting, the steps related to securing consensus and ensuring common understanding may not be relevant. As an individual, you must make sure that you totally understand the goals which you have set and have chosen goals which are reasonable. The key to successful goal setting is the willingness to spend time and think through the entire process.

Like group goals, your individual goals should be based on the values you have clarified. The process for setting your individual goals can be somewhat less formal than the process just described for groups.

First, examine your values list. Within that list, determine which of your priorities you wish to emphasize. Then develop a list of activities which can become a part of your personal activities and which will provide direction in things you do. For example, assume that one of your values is close friendships. As a goal statement, you might list the following: During the next year, I will seek out the friendship of someone who shares many of my interests.

Second, write down your goal statements. Be careful to allow time to develop the list. Do not list so many goal statements that you limit your ability to accomplish the goals. Prioritize the goals list and focus your attention on a few goals at a time. Then, work diligently on the goals that you have selected.

DEVELOPING OBJECTIVES

Suppose that one of your group's major goals included "promoting civic responsibility." The group agrees that this is a very worthwhile goal, but no one in the group seems to know how to go about achieving the goal. One way is to develop specific action-oriented objectives. Objectives are statements of specific tasks to be accomplished.

The first step would be to brainstorm several different projects that might be done to promote civic responsibility. Suppose that the project the group chooses involves an environmental clean-up. Objectives for the project can now be developed.

An objective is a statement that specified the Actors, the Behaviors, the Conditions, and the Degree needed to achieve a goal. You might call this definition the ABCD approach to objectives. An objective might be that a clean-up committee (the actors) will beautify (the behavior) the south edge of the park, using equipment supplied by the park department (the condition) from 8:00 a.m. until noon on Saturday (the degree).

Your group will find that you can specify your goal in much clearer terms if you use the ABCD objective approach. By writing several objectives for your goal, your group will find developing group goals to be an easier task.

Criteria for Judging Objectives

In order for objectives to be effective, they must first be well written. The following list of questions provides criteria for judging the effectiveness of objectives.

1. Are they stated in terms of Actor, Behavior, Conditions, and Degree?
2. Do the objectives promote action?
3. Are the objectives compatible with the general aims of the group?
4. Can the objectives be achieved? Do you have the level of maturity and the resources needed to carry out the behavior?
5. Do the objectives lead to a higher level of achievement?
6. Are the activities varied enough to meet the needs of the individuals in the group?
7. Are the activities limited enough to avoid confusion?
8. Can the objectives be evaluated when they are finished?
9. Were the objectives cooperatively determined?

By now, a sequential order for developing goals and objectives should be evident. Figure 7-2 illustrates how goals and objectives are developed once the group values are clarified. This system can be used for any set of values and goal statements.

DEVELOPING SHORT-TERM AND LONG-TERM PLANS

Part of the planning process in formulating goals and objectives as an individual or a group requires the development of a time plan. A time plan involves three steps: 1) Identify all tasks which need to be accomplished, 2) Organize these tasks sequentially in the order that they should be accomplished, and 3) Set a date for the accomplishment of each task. These three steps apply to both short-term plans and long-term plans. The difference between these two is that long-term plans cannot be planned as accurately as short-term plans. Therefore, a fourth step, the readjustment of the dates for task accomplishment, is involved in long-term planning. In the planning of short-term and intermediate objectives and plans, care must be taken to be consistent with long-term objectives and goals.

Returning to the environmental clean-up example, (See Figure 7-2) the group might develop short-term and long-term plans. The short-term plan might involve planning for a weekend clean-up project involving only members of the group. But the group might also have some long-term plans, perhaps involving a community-wide project. In formulating these long-term plans, the group would need to identify the tasks involved (step I), organize these tasks sequentially (step 2), set dates for the accomplishment of these tasks (step 3), and periodically readjust these dates (step 4).

Figure 7-2

AN EXAMPLE OF DEVELOPING GROUP GOALS AND
OBJECTIVES ONCE VALUES ARE CLARIFIED

Value	Goal	Objectives
Foster citizenship	Foster civic responsibility among group members	1. The clean-up committee will beautify the south edge of the park using equipment supplied by the park department.
		2. A speaker will be invited to discuss the procedure for registering to vote in local, state and national elections.

MOTIVATING THE GROUP

The leader, as well as individual members, can help motivate a group to actively pursue its goals and objectives. Motivation is not something that can be developed by a set of rules. Motivation is the positive attitude that individuals have toward their work. But the leader and individuals can help motivate the group by complimenting or praising (or showing appreciation in some other way) individuals for the work they are doing. Of course, if each group member displays a positive attitude toward the group activity, the motivation of the group will probably be quite high. There will be many times, especially with long-term projects, that the motivation of the group will lag. When this occurs, the leader should remind the members to review how much has been accomplished already.

THINKING BACK

Think back about the relationship between values and goals. How are the goals of a group influenced by the values of the individual members of that group? How do your values affect your actions and attitudes? Why do you have the values you have? What is the source of your values? Are your values changing as you grow older?

What are some of your goals for the future? How long have you had those goals? Do you have any specific objectives for accomplishing those goals? How well do you make long-term and short-term plans? Can you estimate the time a specific task will take?

Do you belong to a group which has goals? How were those goals established? Were you involved in the goal-setting process? How well does your group make consensus decisions? How easily can you listen to someone with values and ideas which conflict with your values and ideas?

These are just a few questions which you might want to consider as you review this chapter on developing group goals and objectives. Remember, the decision-making process is just as important in your personal life as it is in your group involvement. Both processes are necessary if you are to realize your potential in your group, and more importantly, in yourself.

ADDITIONAL ACTIVITIES

LEAD: A Program for Planning Ahead. LEAD is designed for use by the individuals who want to clarify their leadership goals so that they will be more clear and concise about the role of leadership in life. You may want to work with one or two others the first time you do this activity.

LEAD: A Program for Planning Ahead

1. Write down one of your leadership goals.
2. What is the value underlying the goal you have written?
3. Is this value consistent with your other values?
   yes   no
4. Is this value different from the values of other persons you know?
   yes   no
5. If this value is different from the values of others, can you tolerate this difference?
   yes   no
6. Develop a list of activities you might do to achieve your goal.
7. Select from this list the essential things you would need to do to achieve the goal.
8. Write an ABCD objective for your goal.
9. Evaluate this objective using the criteria listed in this chapter.
10. Write out a short-term plan to attain part of your goal.
    a. Identify tasks to be accomplished.
    b. Organize these tasks sequentially.
    c. Set a date tasks should be attained.
11. Write out a long-term plan to attain your goal.
    a. Identify tasks to be accomplished.
    b. Organize these tasks sequentially.
    c. Set a date tasks should be accomplished.
    d. How would you make provision to readjust these dates as time progresses?

This process might be difficult the first few times you try it. It will become much easier with practice. Be prepared to share some of your work with your classmates.

THE DGO SIMULATION

You will work with three or four other students in this simulation project, "Developing Group Objectives." The purpose is to illustrate all the steps in developing goals and objectives.

Step one.   Spend ten minutes brainstorming your attitudes, feelings and values concerning energy conservation in your school.

Step two.   Develop a list of five goals for energy conservation at school.

Step three.   Develop specific objectives to achieve each goal.

Step four.   Examine each of your goals and state what the underlying values are.

Step five.   Examine your objectives. Do they all state the A, B, C, and D elements?

Step six.   Were there value conflicts in any part of this project? How did you resolve them?

Step seven.   List several ways to improve your work in future projects of this type.

Chapter 8

PLANNING GROUP ACTIVITIES

OBJECTIVES

Upon completion of this chapter, you should be able to:

1. Develop an agenda for a meeeting
2. Plan a service project.
3. Evaluate a group program.
4. List potential community resources for your group.

A leader is responsible for the planning of group activities. A good leader involves members in planning activities and in making final decisions regarding the organization, meetings, work, and special activities. Good organization and planning by the leader and all group members assures success in group activities and in attainment of group goals.

A leader must learn how to develop an agenda for group meetings. An agenda promotes maximum group involvement and accomplishment. Of course, the good leader is also flexible and able to change or modify the agenda as necessary.

Activities in youth groups are often service projects or money-making endeavors. Proper planning will ensure the completion of such activities in the most successful and efficient way. Group members will also experience much pleasure and satisfaction in carrying out projects successfully.

A leader will also be expected to plan the long range program for the group. A program includes meetings, special events, guest speakers, and work projects for an entire year. In planning the long range program, the leader of a group must consider the needs of the organization as well as the individuals within that organization. The needs of individuals must especially be considered in assigning tasks and project leadership roles.

The purpose of this chapter is to help you, as a future leader, learn to organize various group activities. As you read this chapter, look for ways you can use this information in the leadership positions you now hold or will face in the near future.

THE MEETING AGENDA

Group meetings can be well-organized and structured or chaotic. A well-organized meeting creates an atmosphere conducive to accomplishment of goals, whereas a disorganized meeting will usually result in little or no accomplishment. The difference between the two depends largely on a well-planned agenda. An agenda is an outline which lists in brief form the main topics of discussion and business to be accomplished. The president or chairperson of the meeting is the individual responsible for the agenda.

The purpose of the agenda is to make it possible for a group to achieve its goals in an orderly and efficient manner. The agenda should make provisions both for the accomplishment of group goals and for productive involvement of individual group members.

Agendas may take many forms, but all agendas should be planned in advance. This planning should result in a brief synopsis or outline of the meeting. A copy of this synopsis should be provided for everyone taking part in the meeting. The leader should contact all persons whose names appear on the agenda to ensure their attendance and readiness to fulfill their roles at the meeting.

Part of the preparation and success of an agenda involves time management. Each segment of the meeting should be assigned an approximate time limit. Members who are making reports should be informed of the amount of time for their presentations. Business should ordinarily be limited to a reasonable amount of time. A guest speaker should have an appropriate amount of time to speak and should be informed of the amount of speaking time expected. Of course, all of these plans are approximate, and the good leader must provide for some flexibility to accomodate unexpected and extended discussion or presentations.

PARTS OF AN AGENDA

An agenda consists of eight elements. The first element is the beginning of the meeting. The time at the beginning of the meeting can be used to create the atmosphere for a good meeting. This is often accomplished by establishing an opening ceremony for meetings. Pledges, singing, and opening ceremonies are three examples of ways of beginning a meeting, but there are many other possibilities as well. Sometimes, a leader may want to plan a game or some other warm-up exercise. These activities should focus the attention on the leader or on the program for the meeting. Such activities should allow the meeting to begin smoothly and on time. As a minimum, the leader must call the meeting to order and secure the attention of all participants.

The second element of an agenda is the reading of the minutes from the previous meeting. The minutes summarize the major actions and activities of the previous meeting. After the minutes are read by the secretary, any corrections to the minutes are made. The minutes must then be submitted to an approval motion and vote by the members.

The secretary's report is followed by the treasurer's report. He/she provides information regarding the financial situation of the group. Profits, expenditures, and the closing balance of the club's funds should all be reported. The treasurer's report must also be moved for approval and voted on by the members.

Standing committee reports often follow the treasurer's report. The number and types of standing committees vary from group to group. Typical standing committees include elections, membership, and budget. Other examples of standing committees include a social and recreational committee, a service and civic committee, or an educational and leadership committee.

These reports are followed by reports from special committees. Special committtees are usually short-term commmittees working on special projects. A special committee for a student senate might be a homecoming committee planning activities for homecoming week.

Committee reports need not be moved for approval and vote by members unless the reports themselves contain motions for action by the group. However, a member may make a motion to approve a report.

Unfinished businesss or previously tabled motions for the last meeting are usually the next items on the agenda. If a decision cannot be reached about certain business, the discussion about the business can be continued at a later meeting or tabled. This permits further thought and study by the members. Tabling also makes possible rejection of a motion without a vote by members on the substance of a motion.

Discussion of unfinished business is followed by any new business the group wants to consider. This is the portion of the meeting in which new projects and activities may be discussed, planned, and moved for action. If a decision cannot be reached, the planning will be postponed until the next meeting, tabled, or delegated to a committee for further investigation.

The final element of an agenda occurs when the chairperson formally closes the meeting. This occurs when all items on the agenda have been covered. This is often accomplished with some type of closing ceremony. Some groups will sing the national anthem, a medley of songs, or their official group song.

Sometimes an agenda will include special items such as special programs, guest speakers, recreation, or refreshments as the last item of activity for the meeting. All of these must be planned and included in the agenda for the meeting. However, they are often initiated after formal closing of the business meeting.

The agenda is an important part of any meeting. Without some formal structure to the meeting, little will be accomplished. Groups that have a poor agenda or fail to follow it, flounder, lose the attention of members, and fail to achieve their goals. Agendas are useful not only for large group meetings, but for committee meetings as well. For that reason, the skill of agenda development should be learned by both group leaders and group members. In larger groups or organizations, it is common to have an agenda committee which, with the leader, receives proposals for activities and plans the agenda for meetings. Figure 8-1 presents a sample agenda for a group.

Figure 8-1
Sample Agenda

Agenda for a regular meeting of the Wilson High School Student Senate, Monday, April 16th, 2:00 p.m., President John Adams presiding.

I. Call to order and recitation of the pledge of the flag.

II. Reading of minutes for previous meeting, Jan Harrison, Secretary

III. Treasurer's report, Mary Kennedy, Treasurer

IV. Reports by standing committees:

> Social Committee, Jim Smith, Chairperson
> Publicity Committee, Sarah Wagner, Chairperson
> School Spirit Committee, Brian Harstine, Chairperson
> Academic Committee, Linda Lockwood, Chairperson

V. Report by Special May Week Committee, Tim Stevens, Chairperson

VI. Old business, finalization of May Week plans

VII. New Business, Discussion of school olympics

VIII. Comments by Mr. Gates, Principal

IX. Recitation of Student Senate Inaugural Pledge

X. Adjournment

PLANNING A WORK ACTIVITY FOR THE CLUB

Work activities are a vital part of most clubs and organizations. The work may be part of a service project for the community or school, or it may be an activity which will simply benefit the organization. The leader of the club is responsible for planning the work activity, but the plans are usually discussed in a regular meeting of the group. One method for planning an activity is the ABCD method described in the chapter on goals and objectives. Another method is to use the following steps:

1. Determine the activity and its goal or purpose. What will the activity be? Will it serve the community, the school, or the organization? Why are we doing it?

2. Set the objectives. What are the purposes for doing the project or work activity? What do we hope to accomplish?

3. Develop the work plan. Make a list of the steps arranged sequentially in order of importance. What things need to be done and in which order should they be done?

4. Develop a budget. Decide how much money will be needed for each step of the project.

5. Assign tasks. Determine which members will be responsible for each task. This can best be accomplished by setting up committees and appointing a chairperson for each committee. However, if the tasks are small or short term, it might be preferable to assign the tasks to individual members.

6. Develop a time line. Determine when each step must be completed in order for the project to be finished on time.

7. Evaluation. Develop criteria for the evaluation of the task. What are appropriate standards for successful completion of the project?

The work plan, described above, should be written in logical, definite, and measurable terms which can be understood by everyone involved. By putting the work plan in writing, the activity can be better understood, and its goals can be more easily reached. The role taken by the leader of the group will be to lead in the planning and decision-making process, delegate responsibilities to committees or individuals, and to do the final writing of the work plan.

SAMPLE WORK PLAN
PLANS FOR FFA COMMUNITY CLEAN-UP

I. Activity: As a community service project, the Johnson City FFA Chapter will clean up Memorial Park at 5th and Main on Saturday, May 18th.

II. Objectives: The objectives of the community clean-up are to develop civic pride within our chapter through a public service project. The second objective is to promote our FFA Chapter, thus gaining public support of our organization. The third objective is to perform a service for the community.

III. Steps to follow:

1. Set up the following committees: refreshment, painting, raking, general clean-up.

2. Notify the park commissioner at City Hall about the clean-up project. Ask the park commissioner for support and suggestions.

3. Estimate amount of paint, paint equipment, and other supplies needed.

4. Plan refreshments. Estimate cost.

5. Set up budget.

6. Purchase all paint and paint equipment, refreshments, and miscellaneous cleaning supplies.

7. Obtain any other equipment needed for clean-up.

8. Carry out the project.

IV. Tentative Budget: Paint $30.00

Paint Supplies $20.00

Garbage Bags .... $ 5.00
Refreshments $20.00

V. Committees

Refreshments: Mary Smith, Chairperson; Bob Kline, Andrea Jones, Don Young

Duties: Plan refreshments and make all purchases before May 14th. Prepare refreshments on May 16th.

Painting: Joan Roberts, Chairperson; Jim Lawrence, Jerri Douglas, Erik Lane, Julie Hedges
Duties: Determine what should be painted at the park and estimate how much paint is needed before May 14th. Purchase paint and painting supplies before May 16th. Paint on May 18th.

Raking: David McBride, Chairperson; Cindy Stackton, Andrew Matthews, Gregg Porter, Ruth Post

Duties: Obtain rakes prior to May 18th. Rake the park on May 18th.

General Clean-up: Suzanne Walter, Chairperson; James Foster, Sandy Ford, Brad Haines, Chuck Bland

Duties: Purchase garbage bags prior to May 18th. Do general picking up and cleaning up on May 18th.

VI. Deadlines: Set up committees, May 2nd; Notify commissioners, May 7th; Paint estimated and purchased, May 11th; Food planned, May 11th; Food and garbage bags purchased, May 16th; Obtain miscellaneous supplies, May 17th; Park Clean-up, Saturday, May 18th from 8:00 a.m. to 3:00 p.m.

VII. Evaluation: Each chairperson should report to the president by 3:30 p.m., May 18th to describe what steps were completed that day. At this time, the president and chairperson will evaluate the task. The task will be evaluated by the following criteria:

A. Thoroughness of job
B. Overall appearance and neatness of the job.

PLANNING GROUP ACTIVITIES

There will be many group activities which will be planned chiefly by the leader of the group. The major consideration for any activity will be the value that project or activity has for each individual member of the group. Planning will help enhance this value. As the leader plans activities for the group, several other considerations must be made as well. A spirit of cooperation should be developed within the group. Members should learn to work with each other in a cooperative way. By involving members in the planning of group activities, a leader can help foster an attitude of cooperation as members learn the importance of individual contributions to successful group action.

At the same time, a spirit of competition can also help enhance the effectiveness of a group. Competitiveness can be encouraged through the presentation of awards and the planning of occasional contests. Healthy competition will help motivate the group and encourage achievement. For example, committees can compete to earn money for the group or there can be competition for community awards.

Communication is another important consideration in planning group activities. Information about the activity must be conveyed to all members of the group. Uninformed members will soon lose interest in both the activity and the group. The leader must make sure that all members know and understand group activities.

Publicity is another aspect of communication. Information about group activities should be conveyed to others who may have an interest or sometimes even a role in a group's activities. Publicity should help gain added support for the activities. Reporting activities in local, state or national publications also gives students practice in reporting ideas and accomplishments.

A leader must learn how to give recognition when it is appropriate and merited. This helps build morale within the group and serves to encourage individual members. Recognition can be given for participation in an activity, for individual achievement, or for various contributions to the group. An effective leader will be sensitive to the accomplishments of individual group members and will recognize these accomplishments individually or publicly.

Finally, a good leader will promote leadership and followership in group activities. Some leader's try to do everything themselves or they rely excessively on a few members. However, a good leader must learn how to provide opportunities for all members to develop leadership qualities through participation in projects and activities. He/she must learn when to exercise leadership responsibilities and when to delegate authority. A leader must also learn to teach followers how to handle the authority delegated to them.

Bill noticed that the members of his group did not work well together. Several personality conflicts were evident whenever meetings were held. After thinking about the problem, he decided that something needed to be done. He came up with several solutions. A) Whenever the group worked well together and seemed to cooperate, he praised them as an entire group: "Boy, you have really worked well today. I am really pleased."; B) He devised a game which required cooperation by several members in a group to complete a task. The task could not be completed without group cooperation. Each group was competing with the other groups, so speed was important. C) Bill taught his group how to brainstorm ideas, stressing that each idea was valuable to the total project. He plans to teach them the creative problem solving process and the group decision-making process. What do you think about Bill's solutions? Will they help improve the attitudes of the group members? What else could Bill do? What do you consider to be the basic problem?

Remember, the activities of a group should be planned for the members of that group. A leader must consider the needs, goals, and concerns of each member and must be willing to compromise in order to meet the needs of the majority of the group. Each activity should be designed to foster cohesiveness within a group of unique individuals.

PROGRAM PLANNING AND IMPLEMENTATION

Another important responsibility of the leader of a group is the implementation of the total program. A program is an outline of activities and goals covering a definite period of time. Usually, a program for an organization will be on a one-year cycle. For school-related organizations, the program cycle will be about nine months in length. Some organizations prefer to plan in shorter lengths of time such as semesters or months. The longer programs begin and end when new officers take office.

The first step of program implementation is to review and evaluate the previous program. This can be accomplished by listing previous activities which were successful and which were not. This step can be accomplished through informal group discussion. The group's minutes of business meetings should serve an an inventory of previous activities.

The next step in the implementation of a program is to discuss the present needs of the group, its membership, and the community. These needs should be added to the list of previous, successful activities.

This assessment of current needs can sometimes take the form of surveys which are administered to all group members or by members of the group to people in the community asking about their special needs or interests which the group might serve.

Step three involves the group decision-making process. The lists developed in steps one and two must be prioritized. This task will require decision-making by the group through discussion at a meeting. The results will be a list of activities, needs, and goals from which the officers of the group can plan the program for the year. The officers, headed by the president, will use the list to select activities, plan meetings, arrange special speakers, and organize projects during the next year.

PROGRAM PLANNING

As the officers plan the program, the following criteria should be considered.

The speakers, activities, and meetings should be of interest to the majority of the members of the group. Providing a variety of activities is one method of assuring interest for as many members as possible. Some members will want educational speakers, others will primarily want entertainment, while still others chiefly want to engage in service activities.

The program should be designed to develop leadership in all members. Opportunities should be given to all members to serve as chairpersons of committees. Members who are involved in the decision-making process of the group will learn more about leadership, and the skills comprising it.

Some parts of a program, possibly large parts, should also be educational. It is important to give the members the opportunity to learn. Provisions should be made to challenge each member in the area of personal knowledge. Guest speakers are particularly useful in this area. However, many organizations have special study and discussion groups which are basically educational in nature.

The scope of the program should be broad. Some groups make the mistake of being too narrow. A science club which only emphasizes ecology is neglecting vast areas of science. A group should try to extend its scope and provide a well-balanced program. At the same time, it must not be broader than the mission or goal for which it was organized.

The program should make provisions for adequate financing. Care should be taken to plan enough profit-making activities to cover all expenditures by the group. It is important to refrain from making finances the main thrust of the group's program as well. It is very easy to gain the reputation of being a "money-eating" organization. Once again, a balanced approach to finances is the best approach. One student group made enough money to support all its activities by selling candy. Another group took on a project to sell plants, but the project got so big that the group was accused of only being interested in making money.

Finally, the program should represent the best effort to meet the unique needs and interests of each individual of the group, while promoting the growth and strengthening of the organization as a whole. This should be the main goal and consideration of program development. Is Mary fulfilling her ambition to become a better leader? Is Tom learning a lot about science in the science club? Is Alice getting a chance to learn more about community service? The program should help fulfill all their needs and interests.

PROGRAM IMPLEMENTATION

Program plans should be printed and given to all the group members. Every officer and member should know his or her role and responsibilities and should be committed to carrying them out. Printed plans help group members avoid disputes later. Orally delivered plans or commitments cannot be verified unless they are tape recorded. Thus, it is always best to have a printed, hard copy record of plans.

From time to time, the program will be changed. This may result in the scheduling of special meetings or special speakers. Occasionally, a regularly scheduled business meeting may be cancelled. When this happens, the leader must keep the membership informed. The leader must make sure that all members are informed of any changes that have been proposed as well as any major decisions that have been made by the officers.

The leader should schedule meetings on a regular basis. Usually, meetings are on the same day each week or month. Thus, attendance can become a regular habit for members. However, some groups alternate the day or date to make it possible for members who have schedule conflicts to attend at least occasionally. However, ideally, all members should plan to attend all or nearly all of the meetings of the group.

Finally, the program should be evaluated periodically. This can be done informally by the leader, the officers, or the entire group, by asking: "How are we doing?" Evaluation can also take place more formally as a leader and the group consider the criteria for program evaluation discussed above. Some groups use an anonymous suggestion box which members can use to deliver evaluation messages to their leaders. This approach is useful to members who are too shy to present criticisms in open meetings.

RESOURCE SPEAKERS

Guest speakers can be very useful to a club or organization. They may bring added expertise in an area being studied by the group. They can provide a way to add variety and interest to the meetings and activities within the program. Sometimes, a guest speaker can bring a new perspective into the group, thus helping to broaden the scope of the group's experiences. An effective program often has several special speakers.

Where do these speakers come from? How can a leader locate potential speakers? A good place to begin is to ask the members to suggest possible speakers. Group members can also watch local papers for names in the headlines. They can also watch local papers to see the names of guest speakers in other clubs and they can look for the names of people involved in charities and causes. They can become familiar with local newspaper editors, radio and television personalities, governmental workers, school officials, and business people. Sometimes, members themselves or their parents or friends will also have expertise which makes them desirable speakers for a group.

Groups should also watch for potential speakers who are otherwise visiting or performing in the community for another group or purpose. Another group may be happy to share a potential speaker or to share the expenses. Such visitors may even be brought in extemporaneously sometimes, even though formal plans were not made for them at the beginning of the year.

The individual members of a group represent a variety of needs, interests, and desires. Each individual also has certain expectations of the group. The leaders of the group should provide opportunities for those expectations to be realized. Unfortunately, this will not occur by chance. The officers of the group must discover those expectations and make provisions to meet them. Without this, the group will experience little success. Members sacrifice time and energy to attend meetings and activities. If those meetings and activities are irrelevant or unproductive, their time will be wasted. Many good members have been lost by groups because they become disgruntled and unhappy with the group and feel that their own personal needs were not being met. The suggestions in this chapter should help you to plan and implement a program which will foster success in your group.

LEADERSHIP DEVELOPMENT ACTIVITY

MOCK MEETING

In this part of the chapter, you and your peers are given the challenge of applying what you have learned about planning and initiating. You will be given the opportunity to develop an agenda for a special meeting.

DIRECTIONS FOR MOCK MEETING*

1. Divide the group into smaller groups that are about the same size. There should be about three to six people in a group.
2. Read the following statement of the problem.

   Currently, our schools are afflicted by the serious communication problem that exists between students and teachers. This is a very real problem that must be solved. It will not be wished away nor can it simply be attributed to the generation gap and then dismissed. Both students and teachers are running scared and both are hyper-defensive about it. Each of the participants blames the problem on the other and suggests answers that involve the other changing behavior.

   If students and teachers are to work cooperatively in a truly productive manner, this problem must be solved. If it is not, students may well continue to be antagonists toward the school. This is nothing short of mutual self-destruction.

   You may be familiar with the reasons why students are rebellious and non-cooperative in school and refuse to communicate with teachers on a meaningful level. Some of the reasons given by teachers are:

   A. Work pressure keeps teachers from having time to sit down and talk to individual students. Heavy teaching schedules and large numbers of students inhibit interpersonal relations.
   B. Differences in ages mean different interests. Teachers do not attempt to find what students are really interested in.

   Some reasons given by students are:

   A. Classroom situations are such that teachers no longer can get to each student on a person-to-person basis. The teacher communicates through lectures to a mass of students who in turn attempt communication through written material.
   B. The teacher must realize that the student has something useful to say, and the student should be able to contribute ideas without fear of being put down.

85

C. Students resent teachers attempting to force them to adopt ideals and morals which will make them "acceptable to society."

D. Students sometimes feel the teacher thinks they "know it all." Often students hear "I've been teaching for some years and I know what I'm talking about; so be quiet and listen."

Although these reasons may have some validity, the real issue is what can be done to solve the problem.

The principal of your school has been concerned for some time about the communication gap. As a first step in exploring the issue, he has called you together to examine the problem. He has promised to seriously consider your recommendations and proposals.

3. Develop an agenda for a meeting designed to study ways to enhance communication between students and teachers. Be sure to remember the limitations and constraints that exist in your school and community, such as the school budget, and established teacher-student ratio, physical space, and so forth.

A. With this description of the problem as background information, your group should now discuss some possible solutions or approaches to the communication problem.

B. When you have finished your discussion, your group should develop an agenda for a formal meeting that might be held to help solve the communication problem.

C. Each group should present its agenda to the rest of the class.

D. Combine all of the agendas into one large agenda.

* Adapted from *Conducting Planning Exercises* by Twelker, P.A., Conducting Planning Exercises, Cambridge Abt., Associates, 1965.

THINKING BACK

Think about the meetings you have attended within the last month. Have they had agendas? If yes, how well were they followed? How effective were they? If no, what went wrong? Could an agenda have improved it?

Think about a work project in which your group has recently participated. How was it planned? What steps did the leader take to get organized? How could the planning have been improved?

Think about a group in which you are a member. Does the group have a written program? If yes, how well-planned is it? Who planned it? How well is it being followed? If no, how well-organized is the group? Could its activities be more systematic through planning? What could you do to produce a written plan for your group?

Planning is a very difficult process to learn. It requires time, energy, and thought. Few groups can run effectively and efficiently without some type of systematic planning. This chapter has presented guidelines for you to consider as you plan your meetings, activities, and programs for your club or organization.

ADDITIONAL ACTIVITIES

1. Select a group in which you are a member. List as many potential guest speakers from your community or county as you can think of.

2. There are many other resources in your community which may be useful in planning your program. Information may be obtained from historical societies, libraries, and government agencies. Brainstorm a list of resources, other than people, that are available to your group.

3. Your group has decided to sponsor a blood drive as a community service project. Along with two or three other people, develop a work plan for the project. Use the list of steps given in the chapter.

4. Reread the list of program evaluation criteria given in this chapter. Select a group in which you are a member and evaluate the program for this year. What are the strengths of the program? How might it be improved? How well is it meeting the needs of the individual members? How much variety is there in the activities?

5. Select one of the following topics for planning and write a one page description of your goal, your agenda, and the steps you would initiate to achieve your goal.
   Your plans for tomorrow.
   Your vacation next week.
   A social event.
   A study schedule for an important test.

Chapter 9

COMMITTEE ORGANIZATION

OBJECTIVES

Upon completion of this chapter, you should be able to:

1. Name and describe three types of committees.
2. Describe how to delegate authority and work to a committee.
3. Identify the responsibilities of a committee member.
4. Explain how to select standing and special committee members.

The productivity of a group depends largely on the effectiveness of its committees, since the majority of an organization's work is accomplished by committees. When work is delegated to committees, the officers of a group can concentrate on leading the organization rather than getting bogged down in details. Of course, the officers must plan for committee work and supervise it carefully. Much of the work of organizations is done by committees or through individual assignments.

Committees are also beneficial to individual members of a group. Good committees provide for the individual involvement of members, giving them opportunities to contribute ideas and to do the type of work in which they are talented and interested. Committees also make it possible for inexperienced members to improve their own leadership skills within a smaller group setting.

Committee work also makes it possible for an organization to provide for specialized activities without losing the broad scope. Thus, a science club can have periodical ecology reports and projects without the entire club working directly on that topic. Members can also fulfill their own interests and motivations through special committee activities. Increased interest develops increased involvement and increased productivity. Committees can also operate much more efficiently than larger groups because they can usually make decisions much more easily and quickly.

TYPES OF COMMITTEES

There are three main types of committees: executive, special and standing. Each type of committee has a unique function in the organization. Members may be involved in more than one. The president, for

89

example, may choose to be on the social committee in addition to duties on the executive committee.

EXECUTIVE COMMITTEES

The first type of committee is the executive committee. This committee is usually comprised of the officers of the club and the standing committee chairpersons. The president usually serves as chairperson. The purpose of an executive committee is to plan and organize club meetings, activities, and special events. Most matters are discussed by the executive committee before they are presented to the entire group. In many organizations, the executive committee functions like an agenda committee. It determines the activities of the organization, but members are usually free to make proposals for projects or activities to the executive committee.

SPECIAL COMMITTEES

A special committee is one which is appointed to do a certain task for a specified length of time. Such a committee is often referred to as an ad hoc committee. Care needs to be taken to form special committees to perform tasks which are not the responsibility of standing committees, unless the standing committee is busy on another project. Examples of this committee might be a decorating committee for a banquet or a welcoming committee for a guest. The bylaws of most organizations authorize the president to appoint special or ad hoc committees.

Selecting members for a special committee is much simpler than for a standing committee. The chairperson and members are often people who have a special interest related to the mission of the committee. Thus, the members who volunteer are highly motivated to do the work. Occasionally, the leader may want to appoint other members to a special committee as well. If all the members are volunteers, strong bias or lack of objectivity might affect the committee's work. Thus, care must be taken to involve a variety of people. There is also a tendency on the part of leaders to select for committees those few people who have been reliable in getting work done in the past. However, this does not permit new members to gain experience in committee work, nor does it allow for the involvement of a large number of members. Careful selection of members for a special committee is an important leadership task.

STANDING COMMITTEES

Most standing committees are named in the bylaws of the organization. Members of standing committees are normally appointed by the president to serve a period of one year. A standing committee usually has prescribed responsibilities and activities. Typically, standing committees are organized for financial affairs, social activities, membership, and publicity. New standing committees can be organized and incorporated as a change in the bylaws of the organization.

SELECTING THE COMMITTEE

A committee will be ineffective unless the right members are selected for it. Members who are not interested in the activities for which the committee is responsible will be inappropriate for that committee. While it is impossible to satisfy every member, proper planning during the selection stage will place most members on a committee which interests them.

The selection process begins by asking the members to indicate their committee preferences. This can be accomplished by handing out forms which list all of the standing committees. Members can be instructed to note their first, second and third choices. This will give an indication of each member's interest.

The next step in the selection process involves choosing the chairperson of the committee. This choice is usually determined by the club and requires careful examination of the entire membership and their committee preferences. Once selected, the chairperson should be notified by the president or vice president. This notification is necessary to determine if the person is willing to serve. If willing to serve, the new chairperson should then participate in the selection of the remaining committee members.

The selection of the committee members requires several considerations. Care must be taken to place as many members as possible in their first committee choice. It is also important to consider the extent of knowledge, skill, and experience each member has. It is important to ask the question: "Which member can contribute the most to a committee and which members would benefit from the experience of others on the committee?"

Sometimes certain individuals are known to work very well together. Thus, it might be a good idea to put them on the same committee together. Conversely, members who do not get along with one another should be "separated" into different committees.

Finally, the wishes of the chairperson must be considered. Which members does he/she prefer to have on the committee? With which members does he/she feel able to work effectively? Are there potential biases or prejudices which might affect the chairperson's relationship with some committee members? These are important considerations in organizing committees. Occasionally, the selection process may require a follow-up interview with members to gain more insight into their interests and skills. This can be handled informally by an officer or the chairperson of the committee.

Once the committee selections are final, the president or vice president should inform each member of the committee selections. If a member declines the selection, he/she should meet with the president or vice president for further discussion and to select an alternative assignment. Hopefully, another committee assignment can be found which suits the member's interests and talents.

After the standing committees have been selected, the president of the organization is responsible for communication to and between committees. The president and vice president must try to encourage standing committees to carry out their mission. Much of this encouragement takes place at the beginning of the year, but periodical "checking up" is necessary as well. This assures the group of productivity. The president must also keep committees informed of the progress of other committees. This helps give a more complete picture of the entire organization to each committee. This can be accomplished partially by instructing each committee to present periodic written and oral reports of their activities. This intra-group communication fosters more group cohesiveness and cooperation and can be very helpful if two or more committees wish to work on a project together. Committees typically give reports of their work and progress at regular business meetings of the organization.

THE COMMITTEE CHAIRPERSON

The chairperson is the key in making committees effective. The chairperson must be able to provide the leadership necessary for the committee to function well. He or she should be a good organizer and should be able to stimulate the committee to do its work. The chairperson is also responsible for the performance of the committee and thus must hold periodic meetings and/or meet with individual members to check on the progress of the committee. The chairperson must not only be a leader, but must also be willing to be a co-worker in the committee. By being an enthusiastic participant in activities, the chairperson can stimulate the other committee members to be enthusiastic and active as well. The chairperson is responsible for the training of the committee members. New and inexperienced members can be taught leadership, membership, and decision-making skills as a prelude to their becoming leaders in the organization.

Officers of an organization sometimes serve as chairpersons of certain standing committees. The treasurer is often the chairperson of a finance committee. The president usually chairs the executive committee. The vice president sometimes chairs an election committe. Officers, however, rarely serve as committee members.

RESPONSIBILITIES OF THE COMMITTEE CHAIRPERSON

One of the first responsibilities of a committee chairperson is to organize meetings of the committee. The first step in doing this is to get a statement of the responsibilities of the committee. It is important that the committee know exactly what their purposes, responsibilities, and goals are. The executive committee is responsible for producing this statement and communicating it to the chairperson of each committee. However, the committee's charge is usually stated in the bylaws if it is a standing committee.

Once the duties of the committee are known, the chairperson must arrange for the first meeting place and time and communicate the information to all committee members. Meeting times are usually arranged by contacting all members, determining their personal schedules, and selecting a time when all are free.

After the meeting is scheduled, the chairperson should prepare the agenda for the meeting. The first committee meeting of the year usually involves an explanation to the committee members of the purposes and activities of the committee. The agenda may also include brainstorming to identify new ideas or projects for the committees, identification of specific committee tasks or duties, allocation of duties, and/or planning for subsequent meetings. Copies of the agenda should be sent to all committee members before the meeting. Usually, it is also a good idea to send the agenda to the president of the organization. This will help the president keep track of committee activities and be aware of the committee's progress. Occasionally, the president may want to attend committee meetings to provide information or advice.

A major responsibility of the committee chairperson is to lead the meetings. The chairperson must start the meeting, lead discussions, keep the group on the subject, and sum up all of the points which are made. The chairperson is also responsible for leading the committee in the decision-making process in order to reach general agreement and conclusions on the matters being discussed and to arrive at plans for activities.

During the meeting, it is the chairperson's responsibility to assign work to each of the committee members. This can usually be accomplished on a voluntary and cooperative basis. When the chairperson does find it necessary to make an arbitrary work assignment, it is still necessary to make sure that the member is willing to do the work. Once the work is assigned, the chairperson is responsible for defining the work assignment clearly and making sure the work is progressing toward completion. It is often helpful to write a memo to each member explaining in detail what the job is.

After the meeting, the chairperson of the committee should write minutes of the committee meeting and progress. This report should be sent to the committee members, revised if necessary, and sent to the president of the club. This helps promote communication within the group and cohesiveness in the organization.

THE COMMITTEE MEMBER

A good committee member is very similar to a good group member. Good committee members try to attend all committee meetings, contribute ideas to the discussion and accept the responsibility for the completion of tasks which have been assigned to them. They will also question activities which they feel are illegal or inappropriate and offer ideas which the majority may not initially approve.

Effective communciation is also important to committee members. They must learn to listen to everyone, to refrain from dominating the discussion, to express their opinions in an honest and straightforward manner, and to talk only when they can contribute something which is constructive for the group. The individual member who dominates discussion can block effective action and cause much ill feeling among committee members.

Effective committees must have members who possess good human relations. They must know how to see both sides of an issue, they must be tolerant of other ideas, and they should be able to work with other committee members. This requires the ability to "give and take," a skill which is difficult to learn, but extremely important to the success of the committee. This does not mean that an individual member should not offer his or her unique points of view, even on controversial issues. It does mean learning to disagree agreeably and settling finally for the majority's view or decision.

Finally, good committee members must know when and how to make decisions. They must wait until they have heard all of the facts and are able to weigh those facts. They must be able to lay aside their own feelings and desires in order to make a decision which will benefit the group and the majority of its members. Good decision making is a learned skill. It requires logical thinking, knowledge, and creativity. It also requires special skills in interpersonal relations.

Committees are a vital part of any organization. They can accomplish more than any single individual can and they are not hindered by the largeness of the entire body of members. An effective committee can make decisions faster and thus get the job done more quickly and effectively. At the same time, it is often recognized that some tasks of an organization are best done by individual members or officers. Committees are best used when group planning and decision making is needed.

A committee is managed much like a large group. It must have good leadership in order to be effective. It must have high quality membership in order to accomplish its goals. Committee meetings should be organized around an agenda in order to promote the maximum accomplishment. Committees, however, can act more rapidly than a large group because they can be more informal and flexible. It is easier to assemble a committee than a large group. For this reason, committees are the backbone of clubs and organizations. They provide an opportunity to practice leadership on a much smaller scale, and they allow more members to take leadership roles in the group.

LEADERSHIP DEVELOPMENT ACTIVITY

In the first part of this chapter, you learned about the effective use of committees. You learned about the various types of committees and about the roles of the chairperson and committee members. The goal of this activity is to help you develop skills as an effective chairperson and committee member. Therefore, in this part of the chapter, you will have the chance to apply what you have learned about the effective use of committees.

You will be organized into a small group and asked to operate as an effective committee in an instructional game called "Committee." Regardless of whether you are a chairperson or committee member,

94

the important aspect of the exercise is to pay attention to the processes (cooperation, delegation of authority, etc.) that occur.

DIRECTIONS FOR COMMITTEE

1. Elect a temporary president of the whole group, club, or organization. This should be done by having someone act as temporary chairperson, taking three nominations, and conducting a vote with ballots.

2. The newly elected president must now pick three members to be chairpersons for committees—a community action committee, an entertainment committee and a finance committee. The finance committee is a standing committee, whereas the other two are special or ad hoc committees. If the whole group or organization is very large, more committees can be organized. Ideally, a committee should not have more than six to eight members.

3. In order to choose committees rapidly, each chairperson should take turns selecting members for the committee from the entire class or group present.

4. The chairperson of each committee is responsible for:
   A. Developing an agenda for the committee meeting
   B. Conducting the committee meeting
   C. Reporting the decisions of the committee to the whole organization

5. Each committee should develop a proposal for a program of activities. For example, the community action committee could evaluate the pros and cons of a park clean-up project, a "get-out-the-vote" project, or a blood drive project. The entertainment committee could evaluate the pros and cons of a dance, a picnic, or a talent show as sources of entertainment. The finance committee could evaluate the pros and cons of a car wash, crafts sale, or a bake sale as sources of revenue.

6. Each committee should prepare to present their resolutions or proposals to the total group.

7. When all committees have completed their proposals or resolutions, the president should conduct a formal meeting of the organization, hear the committee proposals, and conduct a vote on their adoption. Consider the possibility of combining one or more projects during this meeting. For example, a picnic proposed by the entertainment committee might be coordinated with the park clean-up project proposed by the community action committee, or it might be coordinated with a crafts sale proposed by the finance committee.

8. After this formal meeting, be prepared to hold a debriefing to evaluate the activity. What were some of the problems which arose in the decision-making process? How effective and effi-

cient were the committees? Were there any problems with co-operation? Were the project plans complete and practical? What were the strengths of your committee? The weaknesses? The president should lead this discussion and list the main ideas on the chalkboard.

THINKING BACK

What are the most important decisions to make as you select a committee chairperson and committee members? Think about the committees you may be a member of. Evaluate the selection process of your club or organization. What considerations were made when these committees were formed? Who made those selections? How effective is the communication between the executive committee (or officers) and the other committees? Were members asked to express their own interests or preferences?

What are some of the responsiblities of a good committee chairperson? Think about some of the people you know who have served as committee chairpersons. How effectively did they carry out their responsibilities? What are some of their strengths and weaknesses? Have you ever been a chairperson of a committee? How effective did you carry out your responsibilities? What would you change about your own performance? What would you make sure to do again?

What are the characteristics of a good committee member? Think about the members of a committee of which you are a member. Do the members act in a responsible manner? How would you improve the committee if you had the opportunity? What are the positive aspects of your committee? How effective are you in your committee? What could you do to improve your performance?

ADDITIONAL ACTIVITIES

1. Choose one of the following committees and assume that you are the chairperson:
   a. community action
   b. entertainment
   c. finance.

   Prepare an agenda for your first committee meeting and list your ideas for possible projects. Also, describe how you would accomplish the project you propose.

2. You are the president of a new club at your high school or junior high school. The club has been organized for students who are interested in rocketry. What standing committees should be established this year? What type of person would you look for to serve as the chairperson of each committee?

3. Using the information provided in this chapter and in other chapters in this book, develop a checklist which can be used to evaluate members of a group or committee. You may wish to

review the checklist which was given in the chapter on effective leaders (Chapter 3). Use this checklist to evaluate your performance in your club or committee.

Chapter 10

PARLIAMENTARY PROCEDURE SKILLS FOR LEADERS

OBJECTIVES

After finishing this chapter, you should be able to:

1. Describe the importance of parliamentary procedure in group meetings.
2. Show how parliamentary procedure is used in conducting a meeting.
3. Identify the principles of parliamentary procedure.

INTRODUCTION

A major function of a leader is the ability to organize and conduct a group meeting. A procedure called parliamentary procedure provides leaders a way to conduct organized and efficient meetings. The use of parliamentary procedure in meetings can mean the difference between a mob scene and an orderly group. The purpose of parliamentary procedure is to facilitate orderly and constructive discussion of issues at hand.

The development of parliamentary procedure and parliamentary law came about because people who met to transact business felt there was a need for order and efficiency. Parliamentary procedure seeks to protect the rights of all group members in a democratic manner.

The development of parliamentary procedure had a slow growing period. At the start, the rules and guidelines were very rough. This roughness changed with time. The English Parliament established a set of standards for conducting their business and these standards soon became the standards for other assemblies, although these guidelines changed with time, and with the use of parliamentary procedure in new countries, such as the United States. These rules and standards were changed and adapted to fit the needs of our country.

PURPOSES AND PRINCIPLES OF PARLIAMENTARY PROCEDURE

The purpose of paliamentary procedure is the promotion of an efficient meeting in order that business can be transacted in a constructive and proper fashion. If the members of an organization know how to participate correctly in a meeting, they will not only possess a valuable tool of leadership, but their participation will benefit the assembly rather than hinder its operation. The knowledge and proper use of the rules and codes of parliamentary law also ensure that business being transacted will be handled in an orderly manner. The important principles of parliamentary procedure are: (1) only one item of business is to be discussed at a time, and (2) parliamentary procedure reflects the desires of the majority, while protecting the rights of the minority.

Below are some other important principles of parliamentary procedure:

1. All members of the assembly are entitled to full discussion on every motion.
2. The rules and codes of parliamentary law govern precedence in the introductions and handling of all motions.
3. There can be only one motion or question being considered at a time.
4. All members have the right to know and understand all motions being considered before voting on them.
5. Committees and individuals can be given the power to act on various projects without all members working with them, but the final decision rests with the entire assembly.

ORGANIZING THE GROUP

The chairperson or president of the assembly presides over the meeting to ensure proper order and organization. The chairperson does not direct or enter into the discussion unless he or she relinquishes duties to the vice president and takes a place on the floor. The vice president assists the president and also acts as the chairperson of the organization in the absence of the president. The secretary is responsible for the minutes of the meeting and also prepares the order of business for each meeting. The reporter is responsible for public relations. The most important responsibility falls to the members themselves. The success or failure of the meeting and of the entire organization depends on the effective participation of the members.

BUSINESS MEETING GUIDELINES

The efficient, proper conduct of the meeting activities is as important as any of the assembly's functions. The presiding officer and the executive committee play an important role in the success of the regular meeting. These members are responsible for developing an agenda and for setting up any special issues that the organization might present at the meeting. The presiding officer is responsible for proper conduct of the meeting and for following the agenda developed.

The following is a general guideline for conducting a meeting, but this can be modified to fit the needs of your particular organization:

1. The first order of a meeting should be to call the assembly to order.

2. Opening ceremonies should follow if your group conducts any.

3. Minutes of the previous meeting should then be read and corrected as necessary and approved by the assembly.

4. Then any of the officers who have a report that should be brought before the group should be called upon by the presiding officer.

5. After all the reports have been given, the assembly should present any special features. This could range from a guest speaker to a special music program. The reason for having these features at this time in the meeting is because many times a speaker or musical group cannot stay the entire meeting.

6. Any unfinished business from the last regular meeting should now be discussed and acted upon.

7. Committee reports are then presented, discussed, and acted upon.

8. New business is presented and acted upon.

9. When all new business has been discussed and acted upon, the group adjourns. There may or may not be a formal closing ceremony. This is left up to the discretion of the assembly.

Business is brought before the group in the form of a motion. But before any discussion or action is taken on a motion, three things must happen. First , the member wishing to bring a motion before the organization should obtain the floor. Correct procedure is to rise and address the presiding officer as Mr. or Madame President, Mr. or Madame Chairman, etc. This member should also be sure that the floor has been yielded. Do not interrupt another member. Then the motion is presented. Once a motion has been introduced or stated, it has to be seconded by another member. Even then, the motion cannot be discussed until the presiding officer restates the motion and lets the assembly know it is ready for consideration. Discussion on the motion can now begin. This should be done in an orderly fashion, with members obtaining the floor before speaking. Once the floor has been obtained, the members may voice opinions, but they should limit the discussion to the topic or motion at hand and limit the amount of time they speak. After a period of time, the discussion might become repetitious or move away from the motion. A member may then obtain the floor in the prescribed fashion and "move the previous question." This means that the group should return to the motion on the floor and prepare to vote on it. The chairperson must recognize this effort to move the question and terminate discussion if he feels that further discussion or debate is no longer needed. This motion requires a second and then the motion for previous question is voted on. This motion to stop debate (previous question) requires a two-thirds majority vote.

CLASSIFICATIONS OF MOTIONS

Motions are classified into four categories. These are: (1) main, (2) incidental, (3) subsidiary, and (4) privileged. (See Fig. 10-1)

Main motions are broken down into two areas, general and specific. General main motions bring before the assembly any subject requiring the group's decision. Specific main motions involve specific action, such as taking a motion from the table or reconsidering it. Both types of main motions take no precedence over any of the other motions. All main motions must yield to any subsidiary, privileged or incidental motion. Main motions are debatable, amendable, and can have subsidiary motions applied to them.

MAIN MOTIONS

Business is introduced to a group by the use of a main motion. The procedure in introducing a main motion is: the individual obtains the floor, then moves a motion, i.e., "I move that we hold a car wash on September 14th." The motion is now before the body and can be discussed if it has been properly seconded. To second a motion, a member can rise, address the chairperson and say, "I second the motion." The chairperson normally says the following, "(Repeat the motion) The motion has been moved and properly seconded and the floor is now open for discussion." Once a main motion has been moved and is on the floor for disucssion, a number of subsidiary motions can be applied to the main motion.

SUBSIDIARY MOTIONS

Subsidiary motions are designed to change or alter the main motion. Subsidiary motions take precedence over the main motion and must be voted on prior to the action taken on the main motion. For example, one subsidiary motion is the motion to amend (See Figure 10-1). Using the main motion from above, consider the following dialogue:

> "Mr. Chairman, I move we amend the main motion by deleting the 14th and inserting the 21st so that the main motion will read that we hold a car wash on September 21st."

The motion to amend requires a second. After the amendment has been properly seconded and discussed, it must be voted on prior to taking final action on the main motion. If the amendment passes, the amended main motion is then discussed and voted upon (if no further subsidiary motions are made). If the amendment fails, then the original main motion is voted on, assuming no further subsidiary motions are moved.

Table 10-1

Information Sheet on Parliamentary Motions

	May Interrupt Speaker?	Is a Second Required?	Debatable?	Vote Required?
A. Privileged				
1. To fix time	No	Yes	Limited	Maj.
2. To adjourn	No	Yes	No	Maj.
3. To take a recess	No	Yes	Limited	Maj.
4. Question of privilege	Yes	No	No	Chmn. rules
5. Call for order of day	Yes	No	No	None
B. Incidental				
1. Point of order	Yes	No	No or Maj.	Chmn. rules
2. Appeal	Yes	Yes	Yes	Maj.
3. Suspend rules	No	Yes	No	2/3
4. Withdraw a motion	Yes	No	No or Maj.	Maj.
5. Parliamentary inquiry	Yes	No	No	Chmn. rules
6. Object to consider	Yes	No	No	2/3
7. Call for division of the house	Yes	No	No	Maj.
8. To call for a division of a question	No	Yes	No	Maj.
C. Subsidiary				
1. Lay on table	No	Yes	No	Maj.
2. Previous question	No	Yes	No	2/3
3. Refer to committee	No	Yes	Yes	Maj.
4. Amend	No	Yes	Yes	Maj.
5. Postpone indefinitely	No	Yes	Yes	Maj.
D. Main Motions				
1. General main motion	No	Yes	Yes	Maj.
2. Specific main motion				
a. To take from table	No	Yes	No	Maj.
b. To reconsider	Yes	Yes	Yes	Maj.
c. To adopt a resolution	No	Yes	Yes	Maj.
d. To adjourn	No	Yes	Limited	Maj.
e. To create order of day	No	Yes	Yes	Gen., Maj., Spec. 2/3
f. To amend	No	Yes	Yes	Maj.

103

INCIDENTAL MOTIONS

Incidental motions are used to clarify items of business being conducted by the group. These motions must be be acted upon as soon as they are moved since they often directly relate to the discussion taking place on the floor.

Referring again to Figure 10-1, One incidental motion is point of order. The motion is used by a member of the group when another member is doing or saying something that is not in order or distracts from the discussion. For example, if the group was debating the item of business pertaining to the car wash and a member obtained the floor and began to discuss a committee report on new member initiation, another member could interrupt the speaker by rising to a point of order. The chair would ask the person to state their point and then rule on the point of order. If the chair rules that the member discussing the committee report was out of order, then the chair would ask that member to sit down, and the floor would be open for discussion on the motion before the body.

PRIVILEGED MOTIONS

Privileged motions are used to handle urgent situations arising during the meeting. Again, Figure 10-1 contains the privileged motions. The call for a recess is an example of a privileged motion.

SUMMARY

Parliamentary procedure can be a very useful tool, no matter how great or small your assembly or club is. The proper use of parliamentary law and procedure allows for a more fluent and successful meeting. If you understand the terms, meanings, and functions of parliamentary procedure, you will not only be of much greater value to your club, you will enhance your chances of becoming a leader.

ACTIVITY

Now we want you to organize small groups of eight to twelve students and plan a meeting in which you will stage and use all of the motions and parliamentary procedures presented in this chapter. You might reduce the time for some actions such as a recess (take just one minute) and you can have a narrator who says a day or week has passed to illustrate an action like removing a motion from the table. Generally, your meeting or meetings should run from opening to adjournment and every single form of motion or procedure should be used properly some time in the conduct of your meeting or meetings.

TOPICS FOR DISCUSSION

1. Suppose you want to make an inquiry regarding parliamentary procedure and you feel it is important enough to interrupt pending business. What steps should be followed by all members involved?

2. The subsidiary motion to postpone to a certain time takes precedence over three subsidiary motions. There are also three other subsidiary motions that take precedence over it. Give examples of one that takes precedence over it and one over which it takes precedence.

3. Suppose that you, as a member of the assembly, wish to call attention to a violation of parliamentary procedure. Describe how you would handle this.

4. A two-thirds majority is generally required for motions that take away other members' privileges. Name five motions that require a two-thirds vote for adoption. (Refer to Figure 10-1.)

5. There are several motions that are designed to limit or suppress debate on pending business. Name a few of these.

Chapter 11

LEADERSHIP AND SPECIAL ABILITIES

OBJECTIVES

The purpose of this chapter is to help you achieve the following objectives:

1. Identify several types of abilities which leaders may possess.
2. Identify your own special talents and abilities.
3. Plan for the development of your own talents and abilities.
4. Relate well socially to other students of varying types and levels of ability

Leaders are often thought of as gifted or talented people. They may be viewed as gifted because they have outstanding leadership abilities. Thus, some students are viewed as leaders because they are excellent students academically in science, mathematics, or English, and because they provide leadership in a science club, a mathematics society or a creative writing group. Their leadership may combine their special subject matter knowledge and unique skills in leading other students in activities related to those subject matters.

Tom, on the other hand, is just a high average student academically, but he is nevertheless a school leader. He has been elected class president, and he has organized several special drives among students in his school. Tom's leadership talents are general and not dependent on his knowledge of a particular subject. He has developed a number of special leadership and social skills which he uses wisely in his role of leadership in several school activities.

TYPES AND LEVELS OF ABILITY

Until fairly recently, people tended to view intelligence as the only or major index of human ability. Developed first by Binet and Simon in France (1916) and later by Terman and Merrill in the United States (1969), intelligence tests and the IQ quotient became the chief measures of human ability. People assumed that the IQ represented inherited ability and that it was a stable characteristic through individuals' lives. Thus, the IQ was often used as the criterion measure in admitting students to college and in hiring people for various positions in which thinking was required.

Research soon suggested, however, that human mental ability might consist of a variety of factors or special abilities. Thus, new tests were developed like the Primary Mental Abilities Test or the Differential Aptitude Tests, each of which measure several types of abilities. The primary Mental Abilities Test has five subtests, each of which measures a separate and special ability (Sax, 1980, p. 363):

Verbal ability: Ability to use words and ideas effectively.
Numerical ability: Ability to work with numbers.
Reasoning: Ability to use logic in thinking.
Perceptual speed: Ability to perceive data rapidly and accurately
Spatial ability: Ability to visualize shapes in spaces.

The Differential Aptitude Tests are a battery of eight tests (Gronlund, 1981, p. 357) which measure some of the same abilities as the Primary Mental Abilities Test and several others:

Verbal reasoning
Numerical ability
Abstract reasoning
Clerical speed and accuracy
Mechanical reasoning
Spatial relationships
Spelling
Language usage

You can see that there is overlap between these two tests in the tests of special abilities.

Still other tests measure musical and artistic aptitude, creative ability, aptitude to learn a foreign language, or ability to learn to read. Clearly there are many types of human talent or ability. Recently, the psychologist J. P. Guilford has conducted research which suggests there may be hundreds of human abilities (1967). He has presented his research as a graphic model which is called the "Structure of Intellect" and which is represented in Figure 11-1. The cube is three dimensional. One dimension is called "operations" and it represents the kinds of mental operations humans perform. The operations are:

1. Cognition: Discovery, rediscovery, recognition of information or understanding

2. Memory: Retention, or the ability to bring forth information learned previously

3. Divergent production: Searching for multiple, creative or novel solutions to a problem

4. Convergent production: Searching for a "correct" solution to a problem

5. Evaluation: Placing a value judgement on knowledge and thought

Table 1

Structure of Intellect

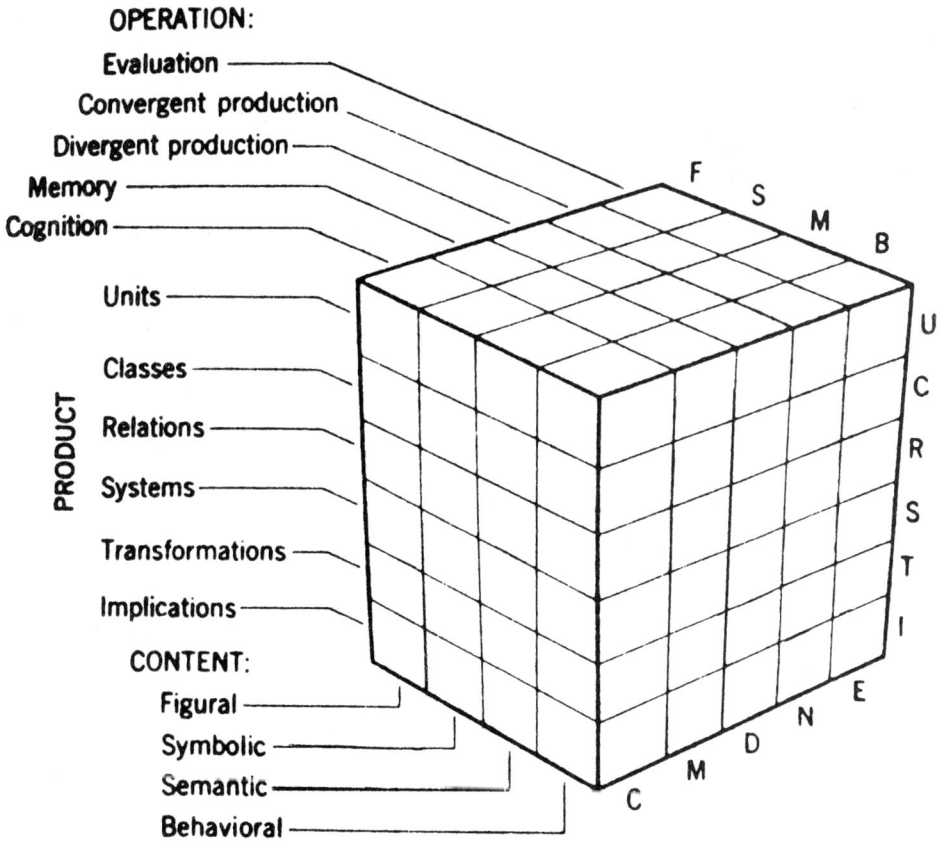

(Guilford, 1967)

Mental operations are performed on "content" which is received in the mind through the senses. There are four kinds of content:

1. Figural: Concrete material as perceived through the senses
2. Symbolic: Letters, digits, and other conventional signs
3. Semantic: Verbal meanings or ideas
4. Behavioral: Knowledge regarding other persons

As a result of the mind's operation on content, "products" or ideas are generated. The products are as follows:

1. Units: Production of a single work, definition, or isolated bit of information
2. Classes: Production of a concept or the noting of similarities
3. Relations: Production of an analogy, an opposite, or any form of relationship
4. Systems: Production of an internally consistent set of classifications of various forms or content
5. Transformation: Production of a change of meaning, arrangement, or organization
6. Implications: Production of information beyond the data given

The intersection of any operation on any content yielding a particular product represents one aptitude or ability. Thus, you might memorize (Memory) some ideas (Semantic) and be able to produce a definition (Units). Or you might solve a problem (Convergent) involving numbers (Symbolic) and produce a concept (Classes). You can see that Guilford's model would lead to a conception of many types of abilities.

Other psychologists (DeHaan and Kough, 1956) suggested that there are the following types of talent or ability:

Intellectual	Writing
Scientific	Dramatic
Leadership	Musical
Creative	Mechanical
Artistic	Physical

Figure 11-2 gives the observable characteristics associated with each of these kinds of talent. Later, we will ask you to use these lists to analyze your own and another person's talents.

Talents or abilities can vary from low to medium or average to high or very high. IQs are sometimes classified as follows:

70-79	Very Low
80-89	Low
90-109	Average
110-129	High
130 up	Very High

Abilities are sometimes reported as percentiles. A percentile tells how many students scored below a given student. Thus, a score of 60th percentile for Tom means that 60 percent of the students who take the test score lower than Tom did. The 80th percentile is high, 90th percentile is very high. Stanines are also often used. They divide all students who take the test into nine groups according to the score level. Nine is high, one is low and five is average.

Thus, you have to view your ability for type and level of talent. Norms are scores like those described above which compare you with other people. You can also compare your several abilities internally and try to decide what your greatest strengths or abilities are.

IDENTIFYING YOUR OWN SPECIAL ABILITIES

Now we would like to have you analyze your own special talents (De Haan & Kough, 1956). Use the scales in Figure 2 to rate yourself in each of those nine areas of ability. For each characteristic or item, rate yourself five if you are very high, four if you are high or above average, three if you are average, and two if you are low or below average. Then get your total score for each of the nine scales.

Your teacher will collect all the scores and prepare a norm chart showing the class average on each scale so that you can see how high you are on each scale in relation to other students. Your teacher will also rank the scores of each scale and show the approximate 90th, 80th, 70th, 60th, 50th, and 40th percentiles.

We would also like to have you rate one other person on all nine scales. Select someone you know who is a very good leader. It can be an adult you know or another student in your school. Do the ratings and get the percentiles. Then draw one profile chart on which you graph your own and the other person's profile. The chart might look like Figure 11-3. The solid black bars may represent your own ratings. The broken line might represent your ratings of a well-known leader.

YOUR LEADERSHIP POTENTIAL

Leaders have a special set of talents and abilities. In this book, we have tried to help you analyze your own leadership abilities and we have tried to help you develop some new leadership skills. Hopefully by now you have become a more effective leader in school and in your community, but you might also have a long way to go to become a highly successful leader. You will have to keep seeking opportunities in school, at church or synagogue, and in community organizations to use and develop your leadership skills. Oppportunities to volunteer for committee leadership or to run for offices will arise and you will have to make yourself available or volunteer if possible. You have to be careful to be discreet and not push yourself excessively at the expense of others. You also have to accept things gracefully when you are turned down. Hopefully you will get some good chances to try out your own leadership skills.

In preparation for such occasions, we would like to have you do a rating of your own leadership abilities with the scale given in Figure

111

11-4 (Renzulli, et. al., 1976). We also want your teacher to rate you on this scale. Then we want you to take your own and your teacher's ratings and compare them, item by item. You should write a paper discussing your strengths and weaknesses as you see them and as your teacher sees them, and discuss the differences between your own and your teacher's ratings. In each case or item where he or she rates you lower than you rate yourself, discuss why you think the other rating is lower. Finally, in writing this paper, we want you to close with a list of suggestions of things you must do to improve or develop your leadership skills. Try to be as specific as possible in making these plans, even to the point of giving dates, names of people, places, schools, etc. This plan should become an effective working guide for you.

RECOGNIZING TALENTS AND ABILITIES IN OTHERS

It is vital for all of us to learn how to recognize talents and abilities in others. Several of the activities in this chapter asked you to rate other people. Those who will become leaders have special needs to both recognize and help reinforce or nurture special talents in others. Good leaders can accept the fact that some of their followers or members have some special talents which are stronger or higher than their own. They can go beyond that recognition and reinforce or help other talented people. Tom reinforces Mary when he says, "Mary, you sure do get a lot of creative ideas for our group." Such recognition or praise not only encourages Mary to do more good work, but also shows that Tom has a strong and positive personality. He is not threatened by Mary's superior creative ability.

Tom also notes that Jim has superior scientific ability and offers to help Jim get into a project with several other students in which they will conduct a research study of students' attitudes toward clubs and fraternities. As a leader, Tom knows that one of his major tasks is to help students in his group develop their talents and abilities so that they can end up being of greater service to the group and realize their own full potential.

Some students are weak or insecure and simply cannot reinforce or help others. They have overwhelming need of praise, recognition or help themselves and thus cannot recognize or help others. Such students rarely make good leaders. These same students may have weak egos or low self-concepts. They do not see themselves as strong, competent or able persons. Their fears about themselves make them negative in their views of themselves and others. They may even be highly critical of others and, deep down, even very critical of themselves.

Think of several people you know, some of whom are good leaders, and try to answer these question:

1. Do they often praise others?
2. Do they ever show signs of recognizing ability or accomplishment in others?

3. Are they critical toward others?

4. Are they generally positive or negative in outlook?

5. Would you rate them as good leaders?

Then evaluate yourself by trying to answer these question:

1. How often do I praise or reinforce ability or achievement in others?

2. How often am I critical or negative toward others?

3. Do I ever seem to enjoy putting others down or humiliating them?

4. Is my self-concept very positive?

SOCIAL RELATIONSHIPS WITH OTHERS OF VARYING ABILITIES

Gifted, talented or high ability students are sometimes viewed with suspicion or hostility by their peers (friends of the same age), and they might experience a need to examine their own behavior in relation to peers. Those who have strong leadership ability are apt to be aware of the problems of relating well to other people of all ages and levels of ability. To be a good leader means that they know how to get along well socially and stimulate confidence in others.

Bill is a junior high school student who is very good in math and science, and he is trying to become a good leader. As head of his school's science club, he is a quite effective leader, but he has also had some problems. Some of the members see him as occasionally boastful and egotistical. He is also quite impatient at meetings with members who are slow thinkers or who make illogical comments. He has used the term "dumb" to refer to some members. Bill also seems to favor members who are very bright or "A" students and to leave less able students off committees. Bill has told the faculty advisor of the club that he realizes that he is guilty of such discrimination and he feels it is wrong.

Bill's mother often refers to Bill as a gifted student because she thinks he is extremely bright, and he is in a special program for so-called gifted students. Some of the other students refer to Bill and others who are in the program as "El Brainos." Bill does not like this nor does he like the term "gifted" which some others students use.

How do you develop a suitable set of social behaviors which make it possible for you to relate well socially to other students and to become a good leader? Obviously, you must become reasonably well-liked, socially skilled, and accepted as a leader. However, you might find it effective to use the inventory of questions which is given in Figure 11-5 to analyze your own social and leadership characteristics and to determine how well you relate to other students. When you finish the inventory, you should discuss it with a guidance counselor or the teacher of this class to get further insights about yourself and your leadership behavior.

CONCLUSION

In this chapter, we have tried to get you to look at yourself and your own special abilities, especially as they relate to leadership. We have also asked you to assess your own social and leadership behavior as you relate to and with peers and other people. Hopefully, you have developed a better understanding of yourself and your abilities and your potential as a leader. We hope that you have set some goals for self-improvement, and that you will become an excellent leader.

REFERENCES

Binet, A. and Simon, T. *The development of intelligence in children.* Translated by E. S. Kite, Depatment of Research No. 22. Vineland, New Jersey: Training School, 1916.

DeHaan, R. F. and Kough, S. *Identifying students with special needs.* Chicago: Science Research Associates, 1956.

Gronlund, N. E. *Measurement and evaluation in teaching.* New York: Macmillan, 1981.

Guilford, J. P. *The nature of human intelligence. New York:* McGraw-Hill, 1967.

Renzulli, J. S., Smith, L. H., White, A. J., Callahan, C. M. and Hartman, R. K. *Scales for rating the behavioral characteristics of superior students.* Mansfield Center, Connecticut: Creative Learning Press, 1976.

Sax, G. *Principles of education and psychological measurement and evaluation. Belmont, California: Wadsworth, 1980.*

Terman, L. and Merrill, M. *Measuring intelligence.* Boston: Houghton Mifflin, 1960.

Figure 11-2

INTELLECTUAL ABILITY

1. Learns rapidly and easily.
2. Uses a great deal of common sense and practical knowledge.
3. Reasons things out. Thinks clearly. Recognizes relationships. Comprehends meanings.
4. Retains what he has heard or read without much rote drill.
5. Knows about many things of which most students are unaware
6. Has a large vocabulary which he uses easily and accurately.
7. Can read books that are one to two years in advance of the rest of the class.
8. Performs difficult mental tasks.
9. Asks many questions. Has a wide range of interests.
10. Does some academic work one to two years in advance of the class.
11. Is original in thinking. Uses bold but unusual methods.
12. Is alert, keenly observant, and responds quickly.

ARTISTIC

1. Covers a variety of subjects in his drawings and paintings.
2. Takes art work seriously. Seems to find much satisfaction in it.
3. Shows originality in choice of subject, technique, and compositon.
4. Is willing to try out new materials and experiences.
5. Fills extra time with drawing, painting, and sculpturing activities.
6. Uses art to express his own experiences and feelings.
7. Is interested in other people's art work. Can appreciate, criticize, and learn from others' work.
8. Likes to model with clay, carve, or work with other forms of three dimensional art.

MUSICAL TALENT

1. Responds more than others to rhythm and melody.
2. Sings well.
3. Puts verve and vigor into music.
4. Buys records. Goes out of his way to listen to music.
5. Enjoys harmonizing with others or singing in groups.

Figure 11-2 Continued

6. Uses music to express his feelings and experiences. (DeHaan and Keough, 1956)
7. Makes up original tunes.
8. Plays one or more musical instruments well.

SCIENTIFIC ABILITY

1. Expresses self clearly and accurately either through writing or speaking.
2. Reads one to two years ahead of class.
3. Is one to two years ahead of class in mathematical ability.
4. Has greater-than-average ability to grasp abstract concepts and see abstract relationships.
5. Has good motor coordination, especially eye-hand coordination. Can do fine, precise manipulations.
6. Is willing to spend time beyond the ordinary assignments or schedule on things that are of interest.
7. Is not easily discouraged by failure of experiments or projects.
8. Wants to know the causes and reasons for things.
9. Spends much time on special projects of own, such as making collections, constructing a radio, making a telescope.
10. Reads a good deal of scientific literature and finds satisfaction in thinking about and discussing scientific affairs.

WRITING TALENT

1. Can develop a story from its beginning, through the build-up and climax, to an interesting conclusion.
2. Gives a refreshing twist, even to old ideas.
3. Uses only necessary details in telling a story.
4. Keeps the ideas organized within story.
5. Chooses descriptive words that show perception.
6. Includes important details that other youngsters miss, and still gets across the central ideas.
7. Enjoys writing stories and poems.
8. Makes the characters seem lifelike, captures the feelings of characters in writing.

DRAMATIC TALENT

1. Readily shifts into the role of another character.

Figure 11-2 Continued

2. Shows interest in dramatic activities.

3. Uses voice to reflect changes of idea and mood.

4. Understands and portrays the conflict in a situation when given the opportuntiy to act out a dramatic event.

5. Communicates feelings by means of facial expression, gestures, and bodily movements.

6. Enjoys evoking emotional responses of listeners.

7. Shows unusual ability to dramatize feelings and experiences.

8. Moves a dramatic situation to a climax and brings it to a well-timed conclusion when telling a story.

9. Gets a good deal of satisfaction and happiness for play-acting or dramatizing.

10. Writes original plays or makes up plays from stories.

11. Can imitate others. Mimics people and animals.

CREATIVE ABILITY

1. Always seems to be full of new ideas pertaining to most subjects.

2. Invents things or creates original stories, plays, poetry, tunes, sketches, and so on.

3. Can use materials, words, or ideas in new ways.

4. Is able to put two or more ideas together to get a new idea.

5. Sees flaws in things, including own work, and can suggest better ways to do a job or reach an objective.

6. Is willing to experiment to get answers.

7. Asks many questions. Shows a great deal of intellectual curiosity.

8. Is flexible and open-minded. Is willing to try one method after another and to change mind if need be. Is not afraid of new ideas and will examine them before rejecting them.

MECHANICAL SKILL

1. Does good work on craft projects.

2. Is interested in mechanical devices and machines.

3. Has a hobby involving mechanical devices such as construction sets, model trains, radios.

4. Can repair gadgets. Can put together mechanical things.

Figure 11-2 Continued

5. Understands mechanical problems, puzzles, and trick questions.
6. Likes to draw plans and make sketches of mechanical objects.
7. Reads magazines or books on mechanical subjects.

PHYSICAL SKILLS

1. Is energetic and seems to need considerable exercise to stay happy.
2. Enjoys participating in highly competitive physical games.
3. Is consistently outstanding in many kinds of competitive games.
4. Is one of the fastest runners in the class.
5. Is one of the best coordinated, physically, in the class.
6. Likes outdoor sports, hiking, and camping.
7. Is willing to spend much time practicing physical activities such as shooting baskets, playing tennis or baseball, or swimming.

Figure 11-3

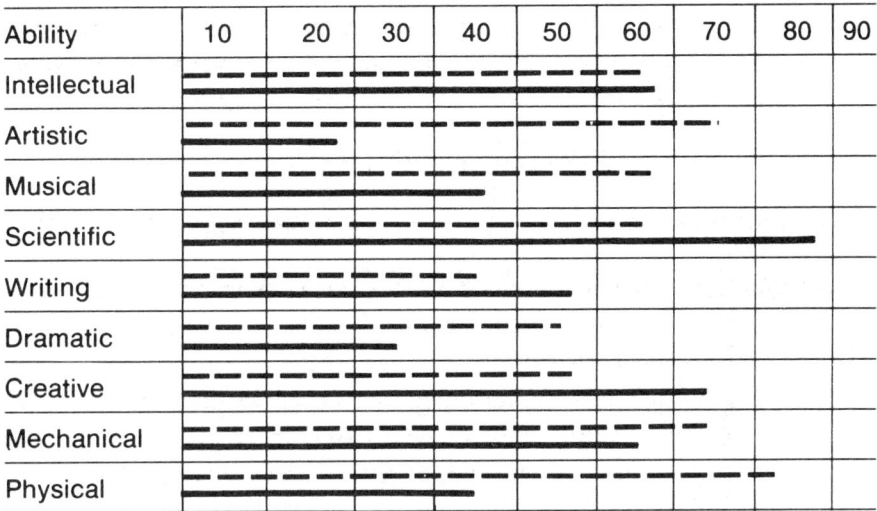

Ability	10	20	30	40	50	60	70	80	90
Intellectual									
Artistic									
Musical									
Scientific									
Writing									
Dramatic									
Creative									
Mechanical									
Physical									

Leadership Education

Figure 11-4

	Seldom or never	Occasionally	Considerably	Almost always
1. Carries responsibility well; can be counted on to do what he has promised and usually does it well.	☐	☐	☐	☐
2. Is self confident with children her own age as well as adults; seems comfortable when asked to show work to the class.	☐	☐	☐	☐
3. Seems to be well liked by classmates.	☐	☐	☐	☐
4. Is cooperative with teacher and classmates; tends to avoid bickering and is generally easy to get along with.	☐	☐	☐	☐
5. Can express self well; has good verbal facility and is usually well understood.	☐	☐	☐	☐
6. Adapts readily to new situations; is flexible in thought and action and does not seem disturbed when the normal routine is changed.	☐	☐	☐	☐
7. Seems to enjoy being around other people; is sociable and prefers not to be alone.	☐	☐	☐	☐
8. Tends to dominate others when they are around; generally directs the activity in which he is involved.	☐	☐	☐	☐
9. Participates in most social activities connected with the school, can be counted on to be there if anyone is.	☐	☐	☐	☐
10. Excels in athletic activities; is well coordinated and enjoys all sorts of athletic games.	☐	☐	☐	☐
Add column Total	☐	☐	☐	☐
Multiply by Weight	1	2	3	4
Add Weighted Column Totals	☐ >	☐ >	☐ >	☐

Total ☐

(Renzulli, et. al., 1976)

11-5

Review your own behavior and characteristics and write brief comments in each box.

Characteristic	Weakness	Strengths	Goal for Improvement
Social skills with peers			
Social skills with adults			
Egotism or boastfulness			
Behavior toward less able students			
Behavior toward those who are better students than I am			
Ability to conduct a meeting			
Ability to plan for a meeting			
Ability to get others to follow through on my suggestions			
Ability to deal with an incident in which a student says something "dumb" or illogical